IRISH BUS PHOTOGRAPHERS

ULSTERBUS, CITYBUS AND LOUGH SWILLY BUSES

A Decade in Photographs 2004–2014

Paul Savage

COLOURPOINT BOOKS

Published 2015 by Colourpoint Books
An imprint of Colourpoint Creative Ltd
Colourpoint House, Jubilee Business Park
Jubilee Road, Newtownards, BT23 4YH
Tel: 028 9182 6339
Fax: 028 9182 1900
E-mail: info@colourpoint.co.uk
Web: www.colourpoint.co.uk

First Edition
First Impression

A catalogue record for this book is available from the British Library.

Designed by April Sky Design, Newtownards
Tel: 028 9182 7195 • Web: www.aprilsky.co.uk

Printed by W&G Baird Ltd, Antrim

ISBN 978-1-78073-071-4

Front cover: The last Lough Swilly bus in service on 19 April 2014 was Leyland Tiger/Wright Endeavour No 521, previously No 1419 in the Ulsterbus fleet. New in July 1992, it was acquired by the Swilly in May 2009 and became the charge of Driver Seamus Crossan. It's shown here on the seafront at Buncrana prior to the 14:00 Derry departure on the last day. With the 18:45 departure, Seamus and No 521 brought to an end the operation of Lough Swilly buses on the Buncrana to Derry route, which had been operated since 1929.

Rear cover: On 1 September 2014, Citybus placed in service 23 Volvo's new B5TL chassis with Wright Gemini 3 bodies, joining 14 which had been in use since 1 July, the newer vehicles actually having older registration numbers. Those vehicles numbered between 2177 and 2195 are fitted with three-point seatbelts. No 2195 is shown here in Royal Avenue, Belfast, on 10 September 2014, arriving on the 14:15 departure from the Stena Line ferry terminal at Westbank Road.

CONTENTS

INTRODUCTION

The last volume in Colourpoint's Buses in Ulster series – *The Hesketh Years, 1988-2003* – was published in 2006. Irvine Millar then followed that in 2008 with his comprehensive history of the Lough Swilly bus operations, and you would be surprised how much that particular fleet changed in just six years. For example, the mostly recently acquired vehicle listed in 2008 was Leyland Tiger No 516; at closure, in April 2014, the fleet had reached, in sequence, No 572, a Volvo B10M/Plaxton Premiere acquired from Ulsterbus in 2013. The Translink fleets have changed in the last ten or so years, too. Gone are the well-known fleets of Bristol REs, Leyland Leopards and Leyland Tigers. Gone, too, is the blue and ivory livery which had been around since the inception of Ulsterbus. And all of the Metro (Citybus) services in Belfast are now operated by low floor, easy access, buses in a magenta and grey livery.

Having finished working with Jack Kernohan on *The Wright Way*, the history of Ballymena coachbuilder, Wrights, a book which received many positive comments and good reviews, I had no intention of getting involved in producing another bus book. However, during visits around the country, and from e-mails received, there appeared to be a demand for an 'update' to the two volumes mentioned in the previous paragraph, so that is how this book came about.

As I've already mentioned, the bus fleets of the major operators here in Northern Ireland have changed substantially. Also, a big change in the last ten years has been the much wider use, and better quality, of digital photography. The photographs in this book are therefore, mostly, digital images, though a few have had to be scanned from negatives and slides when good quality digital wasn't available. At this point, I must thank Stephen Baxter, Raymond Bell, Trevor Dixon, John Durey, Will Hughes, Noel O'Rawe and Paul Rafferty for allowing me to share their pictures with you and, in some cases, for also reading and checking my text. The

Of the eight former Bus Éireann Van Hool integrals the Lough Swilly company put into service in 1999, only one was of the lower height T815H model. This was numbered 006 and is shown here on 23 May 2009 leaving Derry for the seaside town of Buncrana on the Inishowen Peninsula.

1 June 2007 and Citybus Leyland Tiger/Alexander 'Q' No 1476, then still in red and Ivory livery, traverses Donegall Quay, Belfast, en route to Dundonald, in the east of the city.

The success of the *Goldline* operation saw the introduction between June 2006 and January 2007 of 25 wheelchair accessible MAN ND363F/Ayats Bravo 1 double-deck coaches across the network. No 2014 is pictured at the High Street/Bridge Street junction in Belfast on 19 August 2013.

selection of images doesn't cover every change or detail, and it never could else this book would be much bigger than it already is, but I do believe that it gives a good overview of the changes in the bus fleets during the period 2004–14 – the older buses which have now gone, the new ones which have arrived and the multitude of colours which we've seen in the period. Some enthusiasts have expressed to me a view that there's no variety in the Northern Ireland bus fleets in 2014. I would disagree, and I hope this volume shows that.

Time and space constraints mean that this volume can be little more than a photobook, rather than the more detailed histories of the Buses in Ulster series. I have, though, attempted to provide informative captions and also divided the book into what I believe are appropriate, and interesting, sections. Where possible, too, I have selected images of vehicles at work, rather than in depots.

Finally, a big Thank You to Malcolm Johnston and the team at Colourpoint for pulling everything together and presenting us with this nicely laid out volume, which I hope you'll agree does justice to the many images. I do hope you enjoy this look at the changes of the last ten or so years and apologise if I've missed anything which would have been of particular interest to you.

March 2015

LOUGH SWILLY

The Londonderry and Lough Swilly Railway Company, which served the people of County Donegal from 1863 to 2014, has long been a favourite of mine, with its varied fleet of buses and coaches bought second-hand from operators in Great Britain as well as Citybus/Ulsterbus and CIÉ/Bus Éireann. Readers wishing to discover more about 'The Swilly' are recommended to read Irvine Millar's book, *Lough Swilly Buses*, published by Colourpoint Books in 2008.

The last time the Londonderry and Lough Swilly Railway Company bought a bus or coach new was back in 1986 when it purchased a pair of Volvo B10Ms with Plaxton Paramount 3500 coachwork. These were numbered 001/2 in a new coaching series and registered CUI 7167/DUI 257. No 002, pictured here on arrival at Dunfanaghy from Letterkenny on 1 March 2008, was re-registered with Co Donegal mark 86 DL 2748 in January 2006 and was withdrawn in 2008 after suffering fire damage.

Between October and December 1999, the Swilly acquired 11 Van Hool T815 integral coaches from Bus Éireann; three were used to provide spare parts. One of the last remaining in service was No 008, seen here at Milford Port on 5 September 2007 heading for Kerrykeel and Kindrum on the Fanad Peninsula. With the retirement in 2011 of Driver Bernard McGrory, there was no Swilly service any further north than Kerrykeel, though contracted schools journeys reached most parts of the peninsula.

Foyle Street Bus Centre, Londonderry, on 13 April 2007 and Gardner-engined Leyland Tiger/Plaxton Paramount 3200 No 404 is about to move to the stand to work out to Carndonagh, on Inishowen. No 404 came from Clydeside Buses, in November 1997, where it was numbered 173 (407 CLT), but it had been new to Western Scottish in April 1984 as its No L173 (A173 UGB). It served the Swilly for just less than twelve years, being withdrawn in June 2009 and sold for scrap a few months later.

Left: The integral Leyland Lynx was perhaps an unusual choice for the Swilly, but it acquired 20, including two for spares. One of the last in use was No 444, which had been new to West Midlands Travel in July 1990 as its No 1314 and reached the Swilly from Rapson, Inverness, in January 2003. On Saturday 30 October 2010, it was used on a farewell tour which, after a failure, at Umrycam outside Buncrana requiring the liberal use of a hammer on the throttle, reached the most northerly point in Ireland, Malin Head, where it's seen descending from the signal tower.

Below left: When this photograph was taken in Derry on 23 February 2008, Leyland Tiger/Plaxton Paramount 3200 No 415 was in its twenty-fifth year, having been new to London Country Bus Services Ltd, as its TP20 (A120 EPA), in December 1983. It was acquired by the Swilly from Arriva Tees & District in August 1998 and received its Co Donegal registration number, 83 DL 1563, in November that year. It was withdrawn in December 2009 and scrapped.

Left: Seen at Letterkenny bus station on Saturday 21 May 2005 is No 423, a Leyland Leopard, with Alexander Y-type body, new to Western Scottish in May 1980 and acquired by the Swilly in December 1999. Withdrawn in June 2005, No 423 passed in July 2007 to well-known preservationist and dealer, Mike Nash, who has restored it to post-privatisation Western livery. No 423 was the spare bus on Inishowen and was kept in superb condition by Johnny Duffy, who sadly passed away in 2012.

Letterkenny bus station on 21 April 2007 and 1984 Leyland Tiger/Duple Laser No 445 has just arrived from the Milford direction. Previously No 547 (EXI 5547) in the Ulsterbus fleet, No 445 was acquired in November 2003 and re-registered 84 DL 2314 the following month. It gave the Swilly just under five years' service.

The next vehicles acquired for the schools fleet were Bristol REs from Citybus and Ulsterbus. These operated in various liveries, including yellow and cream as shown here on No 455 climbing Convent Road, Letterkenny, on 5 September 2007. No 455 had previously been No 2575 in the Citybus fleet, where it was one of the last four REs in service on 31 January 2004, and was purchased by the Swilly in July that year.

Top left: Numbered in the series originally introduced for coaches, DAF MB230/Plaxton Paramount 3500 No 012 was withdrawn in October 2013. Having served at Letterkenny since acquisition in February 2005, in March 2013, as it was a Northern Ireland-registered vehicle, it was transferred to Derry for the last few months of its service. No 012 was new to the Ulsterbus Tours fleet in March 1993, as No 670, for use on continental tours and was one of the first Tours coaches fitted with air conditioning. In this 3 November 2012 view, it is seen leaving Derry on the 13:00 to Letterkenny via Killea.

Top right: New to Citybus in March 1989, Gardner-engined Leyland Tiger No 460 arrived with the Swilly sixteen years later, in March 2005 and gave the company five years' service. While similar purchases were re-registered in Co Donegal, No 460 retained its Northern Ireland plates throughout its service. It was photographed leaving the seaside town of Buncrana on the 14:00 departure to Derry on 2 August 2008.

Left: With Lough Foyle as a backdrop, Dennis Dart/Wright Handybus No 481, with John Duggan at the wheel, heads for Moville on the mid-morning journey from Derry on 10 September 2009. No 481 was one of just a few Lough Swilly buses to retain its Northern Ireland registration, as it was a Northern Ireland-based company, but with most of its mileage in the Irish Republic. *(Paul Rafferty)*

Right: Lough Swilly No 482 was a Leyland Tiger, with Van Hool coachwork, which had been new to Shearings, Wigan, in March 1985. It was acquired by Ulsterbus in January 1990 and served as a tour coach at Larne depot before moving to the Training School where its manual gearbox proved useful. Purchased by the Swilly in September 2005, it spent most of its time working from Derry, latterly with Driver Paul McGill, but is seen here in the hands of Driver Tommy Doherty deputising for DAF/Plaxton 012 on a Letterkenny duty. *(Paul Rafferty)*

Below: The driver in the picture of Leyland Lynx No 444 (page 8) is Frank Toland. Frank had driven several farewell tours for local enthusiasts, but this farewell, on 1 October 2011, was somewhat different as it was to wish Frank well in his forthcoming retirement. Dennis Dart No 491 (ex-Ulsterbus No 616), then Frank's bus for the Carndonagh to Glengad school run, was used and is seen here above Dunree, overlooking Lough Swilly.

In the summer of 2007, the Swilly purchased a batch of (almost) unique vehicles – Scania N113s, with Plaxton Verde bodywork. These had been new to Cardiff in 1992, but arrived in Co Donegal from Stagecoach East Midlands. No 505 (illustrated) was the only one to arrive in Stagecoach livery, the rest being in Road Car green, yellow and white; it had been No 28637 (J273 UWO) in that fleet. When photographed at Letterkenny on 10 May 2008, No 505 was the bus allocated to the Dunfanaghy duty.

In July 2008, two Leyland TL11-engined Tigers with Alexander 'N' type bodies were purchased from Ulsterbus. No 1235 became Swilly No 515 while No 1249 was allocated No 516, and which is seen here on the banks of the Foyle at Culmore, heading for Muff, just across the border in Co Donegal. *(Paul Rafferty)*

Photographed leaving Derry for Letterkenny on 6 June 2009 is Leyland Tiger/Alexander 'TE' No 518, which had previously been No 527 in the Ulsterbus fleet. Acquired by the Swilly in February 2009, it was withdrawn in March 2012 having spent most of that time at Letterkenny depot as Eddie McGrory's bus.

On 25 May 2012, No 527 (95 DL 6106, *M75 KTG*) came out of the paintshop in fleet colours, the only Scania N113 so treated. It had been expected that it would be used on normal service at Moville and Carndonagh during the school holidays, but overnight on 14/15 June it was stolen from Moville and 'joyridden' round Inishowen, ending up stuck on the green at Malin Town, with serious damage caused to the gearbox. It was repaired and remained on strength until the end, as seen here at Springtown on 19 April 2014.

Five further Scania N113s, also with Welsh origins, but with Alexander Strider bodies this time, arrived in July 2009 to upgrade the schools fleet. New to Newport Transport in February 1995, they arrived at the Swilly via Ashall (dealer), Manchester, painted yellow and fitted with seatbelts. No 524 (95 DL 6103, *M66 KTG*), a Letterkenny bus, though then normally based at Churchill, is seen departing Letterkenny for Kerrykeel on the late afternoon departure on Saturday 26 June 2010.

This is Ramelton on 10 July 2010 and the bus approaching the village from the Milford direction is Leyland Tiger/Wright Endeavour No 528, which had previously been No 1411 in the Ulsterbus fleet. It arrived with the Swilly in October 2009 and, until April 2013, could normally be found on the 'express' duty at Letterkenny. These Wright-bodied vehicles stood up very well to the Co Donegal roads. *(Paul Rafferty)*

Photographed near Manorcunningham on 25 January 2011 when working the 13:30 Letterkenny to Derry (via Killea) is Leyland Tiger/Alexander 'Q' No 543, then the Dunfanaghy bus (though actually based at Termon). No 543 was the second bus of this type purchased from Ulsterbus, where it had been No 1370, and was withdrawn by the Swilly in January 2012 following engine failure. *(Paul Rafferty)*

The last vehicles to gain Lough Swilly colours, though, as it turned out, not actually owned by the Railway Company, but by a member of the owning family, were 18 1995/6-registered Volvo B10Ms with Plaxton Premiere 320 coachwork, again bought from Ulsterbus. Several, like No 563 (left), formerly Ulsterbus No 1627, were put straight into service without repainting, the only concession to their new identity being Swilly names, in black, front and rear. This image (above) of similar, but fleet-liveried, No 561 serves well to show the remote locations in which some of the Swilly school fleet could be found, this being in the foothills of Muckish, beyond Creeslough. No 561 features elsewhere in this publication, in its previous guise as Ulsterbus No 1604 (see p83).

Above: Fresh from the paint shop when I called at Springtown on 14 September 2013 was No 571, latterly No 1582 in the Ulsterbus fleet. Re-registered with Co Donegal mark 95 DL 11334, No 571 was the oldest of the B10Ms acquired and was unique in that it retained the 69 seats, in 3+2 format, which were fitted by Ulsterbus in March 2007. Similar No 565 was registered 96 DL 11334, which will no doubt cause confusion for enthusiasts in years to come!

2013 saw the 150th anniversary of the Lough Swilly starting to provide passenger and freight services to the residents of Co Donegal. The company was actually formed in 1853, but it took ten years for services to begin. Of course, bus operations didn't begin until 1929. This attractive logo was applied to most of the Volvo B10Ms acquired from Ulsterbus to mark this significant occasion.

It was with great sadness that I visited Londonderry on Saturday 19 April 2014 as that was the day on which Swilly bus services ceased. The Commissioners of Her Majesty's Revenue and Customs had presented to the High Court of Justice in Northern Ireland on 13 November 2013, a petition to wind up the Londonderry and Lough Swilly Railway Company. The petition was heard in Belfast on Thursday 3 April, but adjourned for six weeks. Then, on 11 April, word filtered through that the Company had gone into liquidation and that services would cease after Easter. Media reports suggested the company would close on Good Friday, when a reduced service was operating anyway, but, in the end, services ran on Saturday 19 April, and such was the loyalty of the staff, every journey operated, including the Rural Transport Fund for Northern Ireland-supported 22:30 Derry to Culmore and 22:45 return. The fleet, with the exception of the 18 Volvo B10M/ Plaxton Premiere coaches, was sold at auction on 14 June, some for further service with operators in both jurisdictions, but the majority went for scrap.

Below: The first Swilly bus into Derry on Saturday morning was 1992 Leyland Tiger/Wright Endeavour No 540, driven by Liam Dorrian on the 10:00 from Letterkenny. This photograph, though, was taken the previous day as it arrived at Foyle Street on the 16:45 from Letterkenny. No 540 had served Ulsterbus as its No 1424.

Top left: The Carndonagh duty was driven by Liam O'Donnell in similar vehicle No 539 (ex-Ulsterbus 1428), pictured here on the lay-by at Foyle Street prior to working the 17:00 Derry to Buncrana and the 17:45 Buncrana to Carndonagh. The Swilly had re-registered No 539 with Co Donegal number 92 DL 5747, but by August 2013 it was back on Northern Ireland plate WXI 4428.

Top right: Also on a Derry duty was Paddy McCay, with the only Volvo B10M/Plaxton Premiere in service that day, and also the only one to retain its Northern Ireland plates, No 569, previously Ulsterbus No 1611, which was photographed by the shores of the Foyle at Culmore Point when on the 17:30 to Derry.

Left: At the end, there were three Derry duties on Saturdays. John Duggan, mentioned on page 10 driving Dart No 481, was allocated Leyland Tiger/ Alexander 'Q' No 553 for the last day, seen here leaving on the 16:00 Derry to Buncrana. No 553 had arrived from Ulsterbus, where it was numbered 1497, in 2012.

The last bus into service on 19 April was Leyland Tiger/Wright Endeavour No 521 (ex-Ulsterbus No 1419), which was the charge of Seamus Crossan, whose duty covered the 13:00 Derry to Buncrana, 14:00 back, 15:00 Culmore and back, 18:00 Buncrana and 18:45 back, this being the last journey on the route first operated by Lough Swilly buses back in 1929 following the takeover of Barr, Buncrana, then the 19:30, 20:30, 21:30 and, finally, the 22:30 round trips Derry to Culmore. No 521 is shown at Foyle Street just before the last departure, the 22:30 Culmore, with Seamus being seen off by retired Passenger Manager, Connell Diver. *(John Durey)*

Left: Mid-afternoon at Derry and David Farren (Inspector), Liam O'Donnell, Seamus Crossan, John Duggan and retired driver Liam Bradley pose for a last photograph.

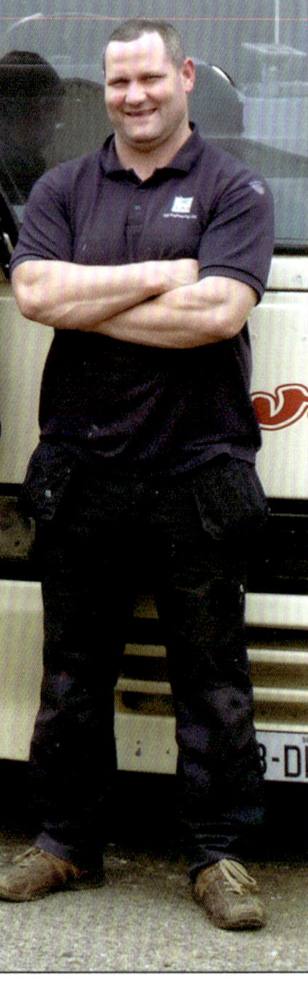

In December 2012, we lost a good friend at the Swilly when Joe Ferguson, the Foreman in the garage at Derry, passed away. Gerry Storey took over the role and, with the help of Aidan, Charlie and Iain, continued to improve the standard and appearance of the Lough Swilly fleet and, it has to be said, that by closure on 19 April 2014, the fleet was probably looking the best it had ever done. *(John Durey)*

Earlier in the week, Letterkenny drivers Eddie McGrory (left) and Liam Dorrian were photographed in the town's bus station in front of Eddie's bus, Leyland Tiger No 554. *(Paul Rafferty)*

Right to the end, the Swilly used elderly Setright ticket machines, as seen here on Volvo B10M No 569, with Paddy McCay at the wheel.

The assets of the Londonderry and Lough Swilly Railway Company, including 47 buses and the inspector's van, were sold by auction at the Springtown premises on Saturday 14 June, raising in the region of £70,000. The sale attracted interested buyers from the length of Ireland, and even internet bidders from Great Britain. Here Leyland Tiger/ Wright Endeavour No 541 goes under the auctioneer's hammer, being sold to Hughes, Ashbourne, Co Meath, for £1900. *(John Durey)*

TRANSLINK:

FAREWELLS

The decade reviewed in these pages has seen great change in the Citybus and Ulsterbus fleets. Gone are the step-entrance Bristol REs, Leyland Leopards and Leyland Tigers fondly remembered by enthusiasts, if not drivers, and which drew many visitors to the Province. The Irish Transport Trust, now Irish Transport Heritage (www.ith.org.uk), has a good relationship with senior management at Citybus/Ulsterbus and has organised a number of events, with the companies' co-operation, to mark the withdrawal of certain types at various locations. In the following pages, we review a selection of those events, some of which don't seem like ten, or more, years ago.

We begin on 28 June 2003, at Ballycastle, on the North Antrim coast, with Bristol RE No 2438, driven by Portrush driver Kenny Campbell, on the last leg of a tour of Coleraine area routes which had also seen the use of Nos 2512 and 2599. No 2438, which was new to Ulsterbus in December 1980, is now preserved in the Edinburgh area by David Cook.

To the opposite end of the country now, to Counties Down and Armagh where, on 25 October 2003, Bristol REs Nos 2454/589/90, driven by Paul Haughey and Pat Malone, were used as part of two circular tours based on Newry. The morning excursion visited Rathfriland, Hilltown, Spelga Dam (where this picture was taken), Kilkeel and Warrenpoint before a lunch stop at Newry. After the break, No 2590 was swapped for 2454, which carried the participants to Crossmaglen, Forkhill, Carrickasticken, Jonesborough and back to Newry.

The oldest vehicle in the Ulsterbus operational fleet at the time, and by a long way, was No 4109, new at Magherafelt depot in May 1978 as No 109. On 29 November 2003, it was used on a routes tour from Dungannon, though, due to a map reading error by the compiler of this volume, the tour actually went international with a visit to Glaslough, Co Monaghan. Back on more familiar territory, No 4109 is pictured at Dungannon Square collecting tour participants after their lunch break. Note that No 4109 was re-registered to WAZ 5652 to release ROI 109 for use on a private car. Behind is Leyland Tiger No 1048 ready to depart for Portadown on service 67 via Loughgall. No 4109 had been scheduled for withdrawal after this tour, but was reinstated, surviving to May 2006, near the end of Leopard operation, having given twenty-eight years' service.

A wet Saturday 31 January 2004 saw Belfast 'invaded' by enthusiasts for the last day of Bristol RE operation in the city. With the generous co-operation of Citybus staff and management, four REs – Nos 2522/7/48/75 – were made available for the day.

This is Twinbrook Estate, on the outskirts of west Belfast, with No 2522 preparing to return to Belfast city centre on what turned out to be its final run in service, the 14:09 service 540 via Glen Road; it was then failed with defective demisters. It was replaced by a Leyland Tiger, which was unfortunate as RE No 2520 had been purposely left at Great Victoria Street depot for such a situation, but the duty Inspector wasn't aware of this.

No 2575, new in April 1984, though it didn't actually enter service until June 1985, worked the 14:40 service 93 to Carr's Glen (via Oldpark Road) and 15:07 return and is seen here in Royal Avenue. No 2575 was on the penultimate RE departure from the city centre, the 18:10 service 35 to Carr's Glen (via Cliftonville Road). It was bought by Lough Swilly in July 2004.

The honour of being the last Citybus RE to depart from the city centre fell to Falls Park-based No 2548, driven by Mickey Clarke, the departure from Queen Street being supervised by Inspector Greg McKernan. The 18:12 to Glencolin via Whiterock Road and Turf Lodge had certainly never carried a standing load, even on its busiest days!

Most of the passengers returned to Falls Park, where No 2548 deposited its passengers in Divis Drive to await preserved RE No 2415, provided by the Irish Transport Trust, to return them to the city centre.

A month later, a snowy Saturday 28 February, and it was time to bid farewell to the Ulsterbus RE (though, as it happened, a few struggled for several months more). Five REs – Nos 2440/595/6/9 and Lough Swilly No 450 – were turned out for a tour of routes in the Londonderry area, with the Derry City routes being covered in the morning and some country services in the afternoon. And in the spirit of generosity shown by Ulsterbus, the tour participants generously donated more than £500 to the Foyle Hospice.

Top: Driven by Stephen Baxter, No 2440 is seen here at Slievemore, at the turning circle known as The Frying Pan.

Left: Followed by Lough Swilly No 450 (the former Ulsterbus No 2581), No 2599, again driven by Kenny Campbell, leaves Altnagelvin Hospital for the city centre. No 2599 later passed into preservation with Mike Nash, Surrey.

One of the day's organisers was Derry driver John Durey, who was driving No 2595, which had received some cosmetic attention to return it to nearer its original condition. The area around the destination box was repainted to ivory, while Ulsterbus fleetnames and 'paperclip' symbols were affixed in the correct position on the waistrail. The location for this photograph is Cumber Bridge, just outside the village of Claudy. As 2004 was a leap year, and John was working on the Sunday, No 2595 was used on city services the following day, right up to midnight!

Two years after the farewell to the REs at Coleraine, on 25 June 2005, an excursion was arranged to say goodbye to the Leopard fleet at the North Coast depot, Driver Davy Clarke doing the honours. As things turned out, this event was a year early!

Top left: The tour started at Coleraine with 1982-built Leopard No 285, which had been at Garvagh from near new and which had only ever had two regular drivers. In fact, on arrival at Kilrea, Driver Jimmy Colvin was waiting to take it back home again. It is now preserved at Macclesfield by an Isle of Man-based enthusiast.

Top right: The tour moved north-east to Ballymoney using No 248, which was later bought by Dumfries and Galloway Council, before No 230, new to Larne depot in February 1981, carried the party along the scenic north coast where a stop was made at Portaneevy Viewpoint.

Left: A change of bus at Portrush depot saw No 133, new in October 1978, used thence to Castlerock, where it was posed for photographs, and back to Coleraine. No 133 was another Leopard to lose its registration to a private car, in January 2004.

Twenty-three months after the Farewell to the Bristol RE event in Derry~Londonderry, on 28 January 2006 it was time to say goodbye to that depot's Leyland Leopards.

Nos 250 and 299 were made available, along with Coleraine depot's No 133, Lough Swilly No 423 and preserved examples Nos 339 and 1886. Four of those taking part in the tour are seen here at Ardmore Church in the late afternoon sunshine. As things turned out, Nos 250 and 299 survived a few months more, No 299 becoming the last Leopard to run at Derry late in the evening of 30 June.

25 March 2006 saw a visit to Newry for a tour again facilitated by Paul Haughey and Pat Malone.

Top: With the kind co-operation of Ulsterbus management, the unique Wright TT-bodied Leopard No 258, new in May 1982, was made available to transport participants from/to Belfast. Under the steady hand of Great Victoria Street driver Raymond Bell, No 258 crosses the river to arrive at Newry Bus Centre. Raymond had been the driver on No 258's first outing in public service.

Below left: The day's tour took in parts of South Armagh and South Down. Accompanied by preserved, though since scrapped, Leopard No 170, No 265, which had carried the group from Newtownhamilton, is seen at the model village of Bessbrook, which is supposedly modelled on Bournville.

Below right: It's a good job the trains were withdrawn in 1955 as No 334, en route to Rathfriland, is parked across the trackbed of the Great Northern Railway line between Banbridge and Castlewellan/Newcastle at Ballyroney.

As mentioned earlier, the farewell to the Leopards at Coleraine was a year premature. However, on Saturday 24 June 2006, it was done all over again – and perhaps better.

Top: While a selection of preserved Leopards made their way north, No 260 was being prepared at Ballycastle depot for the service 178 departure, seen here at Ballymoney Town Hall loading for the 11:02 departure to Coleraine via Balnamore and Macfin. District Manager Jonathan Miller had arranged for the driver's Wayfarer ticket machine to be re-configured to print 'Leopard Farewell' with a sketch of a Leopard.

RIght: Another bonus for tour participants was a second opportunity to travel on a Leopard in service, this being No 271, which worked the 12:20 Coleraine to Portballintrae and 12:50 return. It's seen here running on to the departure stop at Portballintrae. The batch numbered between 260 and 299 were known as 'Specials' because of their superior performance. Ulsterbus had purchased these as a 'job lot', at a very good price, which was due to the imminent release of the Tiger chassis to the coaching market.

The tour continued along the north coast via Ballycastle to Cushendun where, at 16:50, the roar of another Leopard could be heard in the sleepy village as Ballymena depot's No 227 had been specially rostered to the 15:45 service 150 and 16:50 return, replacing the usual low floor Scania or Volvo. No 227 was withdrawn a few days later having sustained accident damage.

Back-up for the tour was provided by Craigavon depot's No 179, the last Leopard in service to retain its VOI registration number. In the capable hands of (then) Chief Instructor Trevor Dixon, No 179, which was new in April 1980, is seen crossing the railway line at Coleraine station on its way to Portrush.

Fifteen months later and it was time to start saying goodbye to the Leyland Tiger/Alexander 'N' type fleet.

By special request, on Saturday 22 September 2007, the oldest Alexander 'N' type-bodied Tiger in service, No 341, new in January 1984 and recently transferred to Larne depot, was provided for the 10:30 service 130 between Larne and Ballymena, where it was photographed arriving at George's Street.

On 25 October 2008, John Durey arranged an excursion from Londonderry using No 368, one of the first batch delivered with coach seats for express duties and then the oldest Tiger in service; it was new in August 1984. These 'express' 'N' types featured an upturned rear window from the Bristol RE body in the first bay in an attempt to produce a more stylish, coach-like, appearance. Once again, the Swilly provided a bus in the shape of No 515, the former Ulsterbus No 1235. Both are seen at Lisneal school.

Left: Five weeks later, and a tour had been planned for Belfast. In the meantime though, No 368 had been transferred from Derry to Great Victoria Street and was used for part of the trip when it covered part of service 107 to Crumlin. A change of bus for the afternoon excursion to North Down saw No 1267 visit Drumbo, Ballygowan, Derryboye (where it's pictured), Comber and Holywood before returning to Belfast.

Below left: The 'official' farewell to the Leyland-engined Tiger took place on Saturday 25 July 2009 when No 1268, new to Antrim depot in May 1989, visited Larne, Ballymena, Ballycastle and the Antrim Coast Road. This photograph is at Capecastle station, on the long-closed narrow gauge line between Ballymoney and Ballycastle. Behind No 1268, driven by Great Victoria Street driver Raymond Bell, is No 1025, in preservation with Messrs Shannon and Thompson, Newtownards.

Below right: The Volvo B10L/Alexander Ultra had served Belfast from 1996 and Londonderry from 1997 as the first low floor buses in the fleets, apart from demonstrators. Derry had received Nos 2751-60 new, so it was appropriate that on 23 June 2012, just a week before withdrawal, No 2753 was used on a Strabane – Castlederg – Strabane round trip. When being painted into the new Ocean Blue and grey livery, the 'Ultras' at Derry received a different version to those transferred to Craigavon (see p67), having a deeper band of blue to the sides, less blue on the front and black beneath the windscreen.

As Citybus and Ulsterbus were making a major contribution to the Olympics transport effort in London, instead of being taken off tax for the school holidays, as was usual, most of the remaining 'Ultras' were kept in service. The oldest B10L/Ultra in the Metro fleet in the summer of 2012 was No 2705, new in November 1996, and on the evening of 23 August was used on an enthusiasts' tour, seen here at Balmoral, in south Belfast.

Top: Friday 31 August 2012 was planned to be the last day of Leyland Tiger operation with Ulsterbus, but it turned out not to be so. However, with the generous co-operation of the managers, inspectors and drivers at Magherafelt and Omagh depots, the deeply rural service 403, the *Sperrin Rambler*, between the two towns had Tigers scheduled to the two round trips. Magherafelt depot turned out a very tidy and smooth running No 1435, which had been new at Omagh in September 1992, while Omagh provided sister No 1436. No 1435 (left) is seen at Draperstown on the morning departure from Magherafelt to Legcloghfin, where it connected with No 1436, pictured at Gortin. Both were sold to Marbill Coach Services, Beith, Ayrshire, in November 2012.

Left: One of a batch of 50 similar vehicles delivered in 1994, Volvo B10M/Alexander 'Q' No 1510 spent its last years of service at Ballymena having been at Enniskillen previously. The few examples of the type remaining were to be withdrawn at the end of June 2013 so on Saturday 29 June, Ballymena depot very kindly turned out No 1510 on the 09:00 service 149 between Ballymena and Ballyclare and the 09:50 return. It is seen here at the bottom of the Hillhead Road, Ballyclare. As it happened, Ballymena depot, along with Downpatrick and Dungannon, each retained a few of this type over the school holidays, being very useful vehicles for private hires and demonstration specials for the Loyal Orders. On 1 September 2013, it made its final move, to Newtownabbey depot, being withdrawn from there at the end of that month.

METRO

In 1973, responsibility for Belfast's public transport passed from Belfast Corporation to the Northern Ireland Transport Holding Company and its subsidiary, Citybus Limited. The basis of the Corporation livery was retained, though the shades of red and ivory changed over time. Perhaps the biggest change in colour schemes occurred in 1999 with the delivery of the first Volvo B10BLEs, with Wright Renown bodies, which were painted in two shades of green with a vertical red stripe. Now, in 2014, the red/ivory has gone, as has the sea green/mint green combination, replaced by the magenta/grey/white Metro livery. Vehicles, though, remain licensed to Citybus Limited.

Citybus was branded Metro from 7 February 2005, though several buses, including Volvo B10L/Alexander Ultra No 2749, received the magenta/grey/white scheme in the preceding weeks. No 2749 was photographed on Belfast's Upper Newtownards Road on Sunday 16 January 2005, proof that it was a Sunday and pre-Metro being with route number 101, which was a roundabout Sunday service in East Belfast, and that such services were replaced after 6 February.

At Newcastle, Co Down, on 18 June 2005, with the Mourne mountains behind, Citybus Leyland Tiger/Alexander 'Q' No 1471 leads a line of three similar vehicles on a private hire to the seaside town. These vehicles were very suitable for such hires featuring 51 high-backed seats.

The change in livery on Citybus vehicles maybe didn't progress quite as management had intended, resulting in vehicles running in the sea green/mint green scheme for at least three and a half years.

On 21 January 2006, almost a year after the introduction of the Metro brand and livery, Volvo B7TL/Transbus ALX400 No 2950, still in Translink green and red, albeit with Metro vinyls applied, waits time in Wellington Place before departing on service 11b, previously 73, to Springmartin, in the west of the city.

By 16 February 2007, Volvo B10BLE No 2796 was progressing towards Metro livery, having had the front painted in the new colours. This photograph shows it in Donegall Square West, about to depart on service 3a to Knocknagoney via Sydenham. Prior to the route renumbering for the introduction of Metro, this had been service 24 (for a short period) and 21 before that.

Left: When the Hightown Road Bridge across the M2 motorway was being rebuilt in 2008, as part of the widening of the motorway, Metro service 1e to Roughfort, incidentally the longest route, was diverted from Hightown Road and Mallusk Road to operate via Antrim Road and Sandyknowes. To provide a service to the affected areas, a replacement midibus route, numbered 15, operated from the turning circle at Bellevue to Hightown Road turning circle. Dennis Dart SLF/Wright Crusader No 651, new to Ulsterbus in April 2000 for the *Airbus* service to Belfast International Airport, was the regular vehicle and was photographed at Bellevue on 15 July.

Below: By June 2012, almost all journeys on Metro local services were operated by low floor buses. The Eastside and Northside Park and Ride services had Optare Solos allocated, but, such was their reliability, frequent replacement with step entrance Leyland Tigers and Volvo B10Ms was necessary. On one such day, 1 June 2012, Leyland Tiger No 1478 leaves Royal Avenue on the Northside service. Believe it or not, but the light-coloured building to the left is a Tesco store. It was previously the head office of the Provincial Bank. The sandstone building is the Ulster Reform Club.

Right: Swinging through Castle Place into Royal Avenue on the 16:36 departure to Springmartin on Saturday 14 July 2012 is Volvo B10L/Alexander Ultra No 2731.

Below: With the introduction of Metro, the Citybus area of operation was extended to include routes such as Ballybeen, Belvoir and Monkstown, previously operated by Ulsterbus. Some vehicles also transferred across, including Volvo B10M/Alexander 'Q' Nos 1524/5, which were allocated to Short Strand for schools services. No 1525 is seen here crossing Belfast's Boyne Bridge, above Great Victoria Street railway station, on 15 September 2011.

Left: Between 2009 and 2011, the Metro private hire fleet was enhanced with the transfer in of a number of former *Goldline* coaches. One such transfer was of No 1634, which, like the others, received this magenta/pink/white scheme. When photographed at Glengall Street on 1 June 2012, No 1634 was back on *Goldline* duty, on the 10:30 service 212 from Londonderry. It had failed in Derry the previous evening and was being worked back to Belfast to be swapped with the Scania/Irizar which had replaced it.

Below: Citybus received its first Volvo B10BLE/Wright Renown low floor buses, Nos 2762-94, in the Autumn of 1999. After a period at the end of 2013 when it was delicensed to the Reserve fleet, No 2762, new in September 1999, was tested and taxed again in January 2014 and put to work at Short Strand depot as the replacement for fire-damaged Volvo B7TL 2944. No 2762 is seen here in Donegall Square West, with the Scottish Provident Building behind, on 21 January 2014.

By 2014, the Volvo B10M/Plaxton Excalibur coaches, which dated from 1999, were getting past their best and, in August/September, six Scania K94IB/Irizar Intercentury coaches, Nos 1713/20/2/5/9/30, new in the Autumn of 2005, were transferred from Ulsterbus, where they had been fitted with the wig-wag lights required for use on schools services. These vehicles also introduced a new white-based livery to the private hire fleet, with more prominence given to the contact telephone number than the fleetname. No 1730 is seen in Durham Street, heading to pick up a contract at the Royal Belfast Academical Institution.

Revisions to the city centre departure points for the Antrim Road and Shore Road services in September 2011 resulting from the Department for Social Development's 'Streets Ahead' project, saw the fleet of four Mercedes-Benz O405GN artics, new in March 2000, rendered useless as they couldn't make the tight turn from Howard Street into Upper Queen Street. All four were transferred to Derry, where they saw use on a variety of work, between January and September 2013. No 3101 was photographed at the former Antrim Road departure stop in Donegall Square West, Belfast, on 23 February 2007.

Top: The next low floor single-deckers to enter the Metro fleet, in December 2003/January 2004, were 16 Scania L94/Wright Solar. No 792 is, though, a 'blow-in' having come from Ulsterbus at Great Victoria Street in April 2011 where it had been displaced by the eight Scania K230/Wright Solar Rurals allocated to the Belfast International Airport service.

Below left: Citybus took delivery of its first low floor double-deckers, Volvo B7TLs with Alexander ALX400 bodies, in the late Spring of 2001. No 2947, from the second batch, was new in September 2003 and carries a Transbus body. It's seen here turning from North Street to Royal Avenue on 20 February 2009, not long after having this bright yellow advert for Brennan's Bread applied. Beyond the buildings behind the bus is a large car park, which was once the site of the Belfast Omnibus Company and later the Northern Ireland Road Transport Board and Ulster Transport Authority's North Street Yard.

Below right: Optare Solo M920SL No 1923 has, from new in August 2005, been allocated to service 95 between Donegall Square East and the Royal Hospitals site in west Belfast. It wore a dark blue/white livery, with appropriate lettering, before gaining fleet livery, for the first time, in the summer of 2010.

Seen climbing the long hill between Greencastle and Sandyknowes on the M2 motorway when on a *CityExpress* duty on 9 August 2007, is Newtownabbey depot's Volvo B7TL/Alexander Dennis ALX400 No 2882. In 2015, No 2882 is still at Newtownabbey depot, though it's now blue following its transfer to Ulsterbus from September 2012.

Photographed on the Ballygomartin Road, in west Belfast, on 14 May 2008, a matter of days after taking up duty, is Citybus Volvo B9TL/Wright Eclipse Gemini No 2214. The twenty vehicles in this batch are fitted with three-point seatbelts, which are rarely, if ever, used. Beyond the bus are the slopes of Divis and Black Mountains, with the television transmitter on the latter.

Citybus played a part in the London Olympics transport effort with 13 Volvo B9TL/Wright Eclipse Gemini, such as No 2336 seen here, going on contract to the London Organising Committee of the Olympic Games and a further seven being hired to First Games Transport. The LOCOG-contracted vehicles had all operator branding removed, but those with First didn't. *(Raymond Bell)*

It was to be September 2012 before Citybus received new single-deckers. While Ulsterbus had experience of operating Volvo's B7RLE model, with Alexander Dennis Enviro 300 Rural B55F bodies, the choice of both chassis and body, the Eclipse 2 from Wrightbus on the B7RLE, was a new one for the Belfast city fleet. The first buses entered service at the beginning of September, though it was December before the last, No 930, eventually carried passengers. No 902 was photographed passing along Donegall Square North, in front of Belfast City Hall, on 4 September 2012.

Also new in September 2012 were 14 Volvo B9TLs with Wright Eclipse Gemini 2 bodies. July 2014 saw No 2368, allocated to Newtownabey depot, working in Glasgow, at the Commonwealth Games, where Translink was, again, involved in the transport operation. No 2368 was one of 35 Translink Volvo B9TLs hired to First Games Transport, a green circle being added front and rear to distinguish between vehicles on Translink's Games and First contracts. A further 14 Volvo B9TLs, again with Wright Eclipse Gemini 2 bodies, were delivered between December 2012 and February 2013.

An interesting vehicle, which appeared at Short Strand depot on Friday 21 June 2013, was this 44-seat StreetLite Max, built by Wrightbus at Ballymena and registered DRZ 9713. It was licensed as a Translink vehicle, given fleet number 2039 and put to work from the following Monday, initially on the Eastside Park and Ride service, but then transferred to regular service, mainly on routes 64, 77 and 78. It was returned to Wrightbus after a week to be fitted with a driver protection screen. Prior to that, it is seen here in Donegall Square South on 26 June, returning from Newtownbreda (Tesco) on service 78. After just over five months' use, it was returned to Wrightbus in December 2013 and was subsequently loaned to Bus Éireann.

It was something of a surprise when the 2014 order for single-deckers was placed with Optare for ten of its Versa V1170 model. Although scheduled to enter service on 1 September, the first of them didn't arrive until the middle of that month. No 1804 was photographed in Royal Avenue on 6 October, its first day in service, when en route from Downview to the city centre.

On 1 July 2014, Metro placed in service the first 14 of its order for 42 of Volvo's new Euro 6 B5TL with Wright Gemini 3 bodywork. No 2387 is seen in Great Victoria Street, en route to the Four Winds area from its city centre terminus in Howard Street. Two months later and a further 23 similar vehicles took up duty, though some of these are fitted with seatbelts.

The final five of the batch of 42 Volvo B5TLs with Wright Gemini 3 bodies to be delivered to Metro in the Summer and Autumn of 2014 were expected to arrive in the green Park and Ride livery for new route 4x from the newly-developed park and ride site at Dunlady Road, Dundonald. Indeed one, No 2196, was noted so adorned at Dennison's, the local Volvo dealer, though they were delivered in standard fleet magenta. The last, No 2200, differed from the other 41 in carrying the new design front, as fitted to Wrightbus' new StreetDeck model. It was displayed at Euro Bus Expo at Birmingham's National Exhibition Centre in November and entered service in Belfast, after modifications had been undertaken, on Monday 1 December when it was photographed on Donegall Quay. Staff have nicknamed it *The Transformer.*

December 2014 saw the appearance of a variation of fleet livery when Volvo B10BLE/Wright Renown No 2783 appeared in grey, with black and white swoops and Translink fleetnames. This 'neutral' livery is to be worn by a small number of buses allocated to Duncrue Street Works as engineering floats so they can work for either company without the confusion of magenta buses on blue routes and vice versa.

METRO IN BLUE

Over time, the fleets of vehicles operated by Citybus and Ulsterbus have become more integrated, resulting in inter-company transfers, particularly when new vehicles are delivered. This often results in vehicles of the wrong colour running where they're not expected. Also, as Newtownabbey depot is a joint Citybus/Ulsterbus facility, it hasn't been uncommon for that depot to turn out the wrong coloured buses in service, which, I suppose, is better than not running the service at all.

The first occasion on which I photographed 'Metro in Blue' was on 11 May 2007, when Newtownabbey depot's Leyland Tiger/Alexander 'N' type No 1267 had been allocated to Metro 2, along the Shore Road. It is seen here leaving Donegall Square West on the 10:38 to Monkstown Estate via Rathcoole. Fortunately, the driver had found 'Monkstown Estate' on the Ulsterbus destination blind.

A major transport operation was put in place for the visit to Belfast of the Tall Ships Race in August 2009. As Citybus (Metro) was a big supporter of the event, the shuttle services were, logically, to be operated with Metro-liveried vehicles. Consequently, a large number of double-deckers were drafted into the Metro fleet from across Ulsterbus, these seeing service mainly on the 9 (Lisburn Road), 10 (Falls Road) and 11 (Shankill Road) corridors. Here we see Volvo B9TL/ Wright Eclipse Gemini No 2247, from Armagh depot, and No 2325 in amongst the roadworks in Donegall Place, on Thursday 13 August 2009.

Perhaps the most unsuitable type of Ulsterbus service bus to see use on Metro is the Scania K230/Wright Solar Rural, with its narrow entrance and 3+2 seating to the rear of the saloon. However, they have appeared, as evidenced by No 486 in Royal Avenue on 1 August 2012 arriving back from Monkstown and Rathcoole on service 2d.

Right: The newest Scania L94/Wright Solar, No 2480, delivered in January 2007, is allocated to Newtownabbey depot. When delivered, it was registered KEZ 7480, but received its present registration, FXI 390, transferred from Leyland Tiger No 390, in March 2007. It's pictured in Royal Avenue on 27 February 2012. The imposing sandstone building behind is the Belfast Central Library, opened in 1888.

Below: In September 2011, Scania L94/Wright Solar No 731 was transferred from Ulsterbus at Larne to the Metro fleet. It ran, initially, in Ulsterbus Ocean Blue with Metro fleetnames appended, but by the end of the year had received a coat of magenta. Come June 2013 and No 731 re-appeared from the paintshops back in Ulsterbus livery. That, however, didn't stop its use on Metro services as witnessed here in Castle Place on 24 June when No 731 was working a journey on service 64 from Abbeycentre.

Top: The World Police and Fire Games were held in Belfast between 1 and 10 August 2013, bringing thousands of visitors, from across the globe, to the city. For those events held in the city, competitors and their supporters were expected to use public transport so services on routes to key venues were enhanced. This extra requirement resulted in a number of double-deckers being loaned by Ulsterbus depots to Metro, as shown here by Newtownards-allocated Volvo B7TL/Alexander Dennis ALX400 No 2327 in Wellington Place on service 26 to Titanic Quarter and IKEA.

The very unusual use of an Ulsterbus Optare Solo on Metro work occurred on 16 January 2014 when Newtownabbey depot, then in the middle of a vehicle shortage, turned out M850 model No 1840 for the 16:20 Metro 1e service to Roughfort, the longest route on Metro. The use of such a short vehicle on the busy Metro 1 (Antrim Road) corridor no doubt caused problems for homeward-bound customers.

The aforementioned vehicle shortage at Newtownabbey depot resulted in some unusual workings in the following week, too. On Monday 20 January 2014, Scania K94/Irizar Intercentury No 1684, which had been converted to 69-seat school bus configuration and so entirely unsuitable for urban service, put in a whole day's service on Metro corridor 2 (Shore Road). When photographed it was about to work to Rathfern, Newtownabbey, on the then late-running 16:28 service 2h departure.

A surprise return to service to service in the Spring of 2014 was that of the six Mercedes-Benz O405Ns, which had been advertised for sale. Four, Nos 2100/2/4/5, were prepared for service and put to work with Metro, usually on schools or the Black's Road Park and Ride service, No 2101 returning to Derry and No 2103 being allocated there, though it never actually left Belfast. No 2100 is seen here on Donegall Quay, heading for George Best Belfast City Airport.

We've looked at blue buses on Metro services, but the reverse is also true, with examples in magenta appearing on Ulsterbus routes.

Right: This rural location is Milltown, between Lisburn and Derriaghy on 17 August 2007. The bus is Volvo B7TL No 2936, which was then working from Ulsterbus' Great Victoria Street depot. Although delivered to Citybus in that concern's colours in October 2001 (see *Buses in Ulster Vol 6: Citybus and Ulsterbus, The Hesketh Years*, p82, Colourpoint Books 2006), it didn't enter service and was almost immediately transferred to Ulsterbus. In preparation for return to Citybus from 1 September 2007, it was repainted in early August, but retained by Ulsterbus, resulting in photo opportunities such as this.

Below: With the delivery to Citybus of 14 new Volvo B9TL/Wright Gemini 2s in September 2012, further Volvo B7TL/Alexander Dennis ALX400s were cascaded to Ulsterbus. No 2879 was transferred to Craigavon depot and is seen here leaving Belfast on the 15:00 departure on service 51 to Lisburn, Moira, Lurgan and Craigavon on 7 September 2012.

Top: Seen at Altnagelvin Hospital, Londonderry, on 22 September 2012, with Driver John Durey at the wheel, and showing no sign of its allegiance, is Ulsterbus Mercedes-Benz O405N No 2105, not long transferred to The Maiden City. The six O405Ns, new in February 2000, proved popular buses at Derry, at least with drivers. All were repainted blue by Christmas 2012, and withdrawn in June 2013! However, in the Spring of 2014, a requirement for additional vehicles saw one of them, No 2101, returned to service in Derry.

Left: Transferred from Citybus at Short Strand to the reserve fleet at the end of December 2012, Volvo B10M/Alexander 'Q' No 1525 was quickly returned to use with Ulsterbus at Downpatrick. When seen on 8 February 2013, it appeared to be suffering an identity crisis with the nearside partly in blue, though with Metro magenta vinyls on the cantrail, and the offside in magenta. Perhaps it was being painted between journeys? Its appearance certainly did nothing to promote the image of quality which I'm sure Translink management would wish to see.

ULSTERBUS

The Ulsterbus fleet has changed considerably in the decade reviewed. In late Spring 2013, the Leyland marque became extinct, and the step-entrance service bus (high-capacity vehicles excluded) wasn't far behind due to the huge influx of low floor, easy access, Scania and Volvo types. The double-decker has also made a return to the fleet, with batches of Alexander Dennis ALX400-bodied Volvo B7TLs delivered new, similar vehicles transferred in from Citybus, and 80 new Volvo B9TLs with Wright's stylish Eclipse Gemini bodywork. The first sixteen photographs show types which have left the Company's service (or are just about to).

The Dennis Dart in the Citybus and Ulsterbus fleets wasn't the success it appears to have been in fleets in Great Britain. More than half of the fleet delivered in 1994 passed to the Londonderry and Lough Swilly Railway Company in, where they operated successfully Co Donegal, though No 602, seen at Coleraine on 25 June 2005, wasn't one of those.

After service in Belfast with Citybus, some of the Gardner-engined Leyland Tigers with Alexander 'N' type bodies were transferred to Ulsterbus. One such vehicle was No 2610, new in June 1988 and which joined the Ulsterbus fleet in September 2004. Unusually, on the evening of 29 June 2007, No 2610 was allocated to a late turn at Derry and is pictured at Goshaden about to return to the city on service 147.

In November/December 1988, ten Leyland Tigers, Nos 1200-9, were delivered for use on Derry City services. They had 48 seats, instead of the usual 53, with a standing area and luggage pen. On 2 August 2008, No 1205 was photographed at Claudy working a country run to the village of Park.

The Alexander 'N'type-bodied Leyland Tigers, with Volvo engines, allocated to Ballymena depot were popular buses with the drivers there. On Saturday 24 October 2009, No 1311, new in February 1990, was found on the 15:45 service 120 between Ballymena and Antrim, and seen at the latter place. Antrim is a perfect example of bus and rail interchange, just perhaps not integration, with both modes serving the same site. A new interchange on the same site opened in 2013.

In 2010, Volvo-engined Leyland Tiger/Alexander 'N' type No 1335, which had been at Newry since new in June 1990, was transferred to Ballymena, where it became a very popular bus. By special request, on 30 June 2010, the day it was scheduled for withdrawal (though it actually ran until the end of the school summer holidays), it was allocated to the 15:45 Ballymena to Limavady run and is seen here in Church Street, Kilrea, with St Patrick's Church beyond. On withdrawal No 1335 was purchased by the cycling club based at Falls Park depot, but sold in late 2014.

Top: The first Volvo B10Ms for the Ulsterbus Tours fleet were two – Nos 504/5 – new in April 1994. They had 47 seats and toilets, to provide more comfort for passengers on the company's programme of continental tours. After almost ten years on Tours work, No 504 was transferred to Lisburn as a depot coach, for private hire and contracts, then four years later, in April 2008, it was on the move again, this time to the Driving School where it was given this special livery. It served as a training vehicle for just over twenty-one months, during which period it was re-numbered 2504, before being withdrawn at the end of January 2010 and sold to McGonagle, Buncrana, Co Donegal, where it was re-registered 94 DL 6206.

A regular Saturday morning working for a Tiger in Belfast in Summer 2010 was the 10:30 service 15 to Downpatrick. As this journey, worked from Downpatrick depot's outstation at Ardglass, ran into Belfast via the Annacloy route, which has a weight restriction at Kilmore bridge preventing the use of heavier, low floor types, a Tiger, or Volvo B10M, was essential. No 1368, new in June 1991, is seen passing along Donegall Square North, Belfast, on 19 June.

Wright Endeavour-bodied Leyland Tiger No 1415 was new in June 1992 as a 53-seat *Goldline* coach. Later re-seated with 57 high-backed bus seats for use on schools duties, it was sold, in October 2009, to Lough Swilly, becoming No 529 in that fleet, subsequently being re-registered in Co Donegal as 92 DL 5728. This photograph, taken in Royal Avenue, Belfast, on 29 April 2009, shows No 1415 in bus livery, when it was allocated to Newtownabbey Depot.

As they were replaced in the Citybus fleet by new low floor double and single-deckers, the Alexander 'Q' type-bodied Leyland Tigers were painted blue and transferred to the Ulsterbus fleet to displace older Tigers there. No 1462, new to Citybus in November 1992 and transferred to Ulsterbus in November 2005, was working from Newcastle depot when photographed in Belfast on 22 July 2010.

No 2640 had been transferred from Citybus to Ulsterbus in October 2005 and was working from Craigavon depot when photographed crossing Belfast's Boyne Bridge on 11 June 2010. No 2640, as can be seen on page 119, was later converted for use by the engineers at Duncrue Street Works.

30 June 2011 and Ballymena depot withdrew three buses which had spent their entire service at the depot having been new in January (1483/5) and February 1993 (1484). No 1485 worked the last journey, the 15:45 service 150 to Cushendun and 16:50 return. All three were quickly removed to Great Victoria Street depot, where they are seen a few days later. They were sold to Dodds, Ayr, for further service.

Top left: It's just after 11:00 on 31 August 2011 and the last Leyland Tiger delivered to Ulsterbus, No 1500, is seen leaving Belfast's Europa Bus Centre on its last journey to its base at Craigavon. Scheduled for withdrawal on its arrival back, it was quickly reinstated at Armagh and later reached Enniskillen for a short period before being transferred to the Reserve Fleet.

Top right: The Volvo B10L/Alexander Ultra fleet had been divided between Citybus (50 production examples plus two demonstrators) and Ulsterbus (10 production examples) at Londonderry. In October and November 2005, several surplus examples from the Citybus fleet were, surprisingly, transferred to Craigavon depot. On 6 June 2007, No 2742, freshly repainted in Ocean Blue/grey/white, waits at the Glengall Street/Boyne Bridge junction, Belfast, when on the 16:00 service 51 departure.

Right: This is the Co Antrim seaside town of Carnlough, hometown, for those interested in football, of Liverpool FC manager, Brendan Rodgers. Probably of more interest to readers of this volume is Optare Solo M850 No 1819, one of ten purchased in Spring 2000 for use on rural services. It's 18 April 2009, and No 1819 is ready to return to Larne on service 162, and not 154½ as shown on the route number display! No 1819 was withdrawn for disposal just a couple of weeks after this picture was taken.

The 'Ultras' at Londonderry received a different livery to those at Craigavon, having a deeper band of blue to the sides, less blue on the front and black beneath the windscreen. The last of them to go from Pennyburn garage, Derry, was No 2759, which was removed, for scrap, by Hamill, Ahoghill, during the evening of Friday 10 May 2013. It was lifted by forklift then placed on a lowloader for the journey to the scrapyard. *(John Durey)*

Seventy-eight years of Leyland bus operation by the state-owned transport operators in Northern Ireland came to an end on Friday 17 May 2013 when the last Leyland Tiger in public service, No 1489, was withdrawn at Downpatrick. The occasion passed without ceremony, and it's not even certain that No 1489 was actually used that day. It was in use, though, on 23 April when it was photographed passing through Donegall Square North, Belfast on the 10:30 service 15a to Downpatrick.

Something else which disappeared during the decade under review was the mint green/sea green livery introduced with the arrival of the Volvo B10BLE/Wright Renowns in 1999/2000.

Top: Parked in the lay-over area at Foyle Street Bus Centre, Londonderry, on 24 September 2005, Volvo B10L/ Alexander Ultra No 2753 is in the simplified version of Translink's low floor livery, without the mint green swoop. It has also received the latest fleetname and logo styles and been fitted with a replacement, LED, destination display.

Right: Newtownards-based Volvo B10BLE No 2833, new in February 2000 and shown passing along Belfast's Oxford Street on 26 June 2007, is also in the simplified version of the low floor livery.

We now take a look at the various types of bus that could be seen in the Ulsterbus fleet during 2014.

18 September 2014 and Volvo B10BLE/Wright Renown No 2835 heads along Oxford Street, Belfast, en route to its home depot at Newtownards. No 2835 is unique in the Volvo B10BLE fleet by virtue of having been fitted with LED destination and route number displays.

Service 131 runs between Ballymena and Ballycastle via Cloughmills, with journeys worked from either end. However, on Saturdays, at least until the end of August 2013, the 11:50 journey from Ballymena to Cloughmills and 12:25 return was a Larne operation; this journey has since been withdrawn. On 24 September 2011, 2003-built Scania L94/ Wright Solar No 771 was the allocated bus. On its return to Ballymena it would run to Carnlough on service 128 at 13:10 then 'light' back to Larne depot. *(Noel O'Rawe)*

In the last few years, Optare Solo No 1854, new in May 2003 and scheduled for replacement in the Autumn of 2014, has been a bit of a nomad having worked at Coleraine, Newtownabbey, Lisburn and Newcastle. Here, on 19 August 2014, it's seen arriving at the hamlet of Attical, high in the Mourne Mountains, when working on service 407 the *Kilkeel Rambler* from the Co Down fishing port. At Attical, on Tuesdays to Fridays between the beginning of May and the end of August, services 407 and 405 the *Mourne Rambler* from Newcastle connected to provide enhanced opportunities for visitors to enjoy the mountain scenery.

April/May 2011 saw the replacement of the 2006 Scania L94/Wright Solar buses, Nos 819-24, on the service between the Europa Bus Centre and Belfast International Airport. These vehicles had accumulated substantial mileages and had suffered a pounding during the widening works on the M2 motorway. No 822 had been stripped of its *Airport Express 300* vinyls when photographed at High Street, Belfast, on 4 May 2011.

The later vehicles in this batch were numbered from 2401 to 2480 and most received three-digit registration numbers transferred from about-to-be-withdrawn Leyland Tigers. No 2402, allocated new to Newtownards depot in August 2006, is such an example; FXI 402 was previously on Tiger No 402. It was photographed at Donaghadee, heading for Bangor on service 3, on 22 June 2013.

Northern Ireland was to be the last region of the United Kingdom to switch from analogue to digital television, the final changeover taking place on 24 October 2012. To increase public awareness of the impending change, in July, Ulsterbus Volvo B7TL/Alexander Dennis No 2301, based at Londonderry depot, was given an appropriate vinyl wrap. It was photographed leaving Derry for Limavady on 4 August 2012. Citybus (Metro) No 2898 was similarly adorned.'

The transfer of double-deckers from Citybus to Ulsterbus, ostensibly to enhance the efficiency of schools services, produced the odd conversion of a normal service journey to double-deck operation. One such journey in the late Spring of 2012 was the 17:45 Ballymena to Ballycastle service 131, photographed here on 11 May when ex-Citybus Volvo B7TL/Alexander Dennis No 2984 was in use from Ballycastle depot. *(Noel O'Rawe)*

Left: By September 2014, all but three of the Volvo B7TL/Alexander ALX400s delivered to Citybus in the Spring of 2001 had been delicensed to reserve or, in the case of No 2927, withdrawn after being hijacked and burned back in 2005 (see p115). It was therefore something of a surprise when several members of this batch were relicensed and transferred to Ulsterbus for schools duties. Further excitement was caused in the enthusiast community when several, such as Derry depot's No 2928, seen here at Culmore Point on 4 October, appeared in the Ocean Blue and grey livery.

Below: The 2014 Commonwealth Games were held in Glasgow and, as with the Olympic Games in London in 2012, Translink supplied buses from both the Metro (as seen on p49) and Ulsterbus fleets on contract to the Games organisers and on hire to First Games Transport. Ninety-two Volvo B9TLs were shipped on Stena Line, to Loch Ryan Port, in south-west Scotland, on 9 and 13 July. No 2241, normally based at Londonderry, is seen here on 29 July leaving the Games Transport Hub at Dalmarnock, Glasgow.

Introduced in 2002, it was to be 2007 before the Wright Gemini body entered the Ulsterbus fleet, when 80 Eclipse Gemini models, on the Volvo B9TL chassis, were delivered. The 80 were spread across the company, the only depots not to receive an allocation being Craigavon and Enniskillen. The summer of 2012 was a busy time for Ulsterbus, with the Diamond Jubilee visit of Her Majesty Queen Elizabeth II, the Irish Open Golf at Royal Portrush and the preparation and movement of vehicles to London for the Olympic Games contracts. HM The Queen's visit and the Irish Open were back to back at the end of June so a fleet of around 70 buses was assembled to provide Park and Ride services at both events. At the other end of the Province to where you'd normally find it operating, Armagh depot's Volvo B9TL No 2270 arrives at a very wet Portrush to take up duty on one of the several Park and Ride services operated in connection with the golf competition.

By the end of 2012, the six Mercedes O405Ns transferred from Citybus to Ulsterbus at Londonderry in September had lost their Metro magenta for Ulsterbus Ocean Blue. No 2102 was photographed on Strand Road on 2 February 2013 returning from Slievemore. It was in this general area that the Londonderry and Lough Swilly Railway crossed en route from the station at Graving Dock to Pennyburn and on to Tooban Junction, Letterkenny, Buncrana and Carndonagh. The Lough Swilly's Pennyburn premises were where the white building to the left of No 2102 now stands. In 2014, No 2102 was actually working for Metro, albeit in blue, but similar No 2101 served the residents of the Maiden City until the end of June.

In the early summer of 2013, just in time for the G8 Summit held at the Lough Erne Resort in Co Fermanagh on 17/18 June, Ulsterbus took delivery of the first of a batch of 23 Irizar i4-bodied Scania K320s, Nos 601-23 (NFZ 9601-23). These differed from previous deliveries with this chassis/body combination in that they weren't to *Goldline* specification, but to what Ulsterbus referred to as 'interurban'. In effect, they are true dual-purpose vehicles, with 55, high-backed, fixed seats in a coach shell. The first ten were initially allocated to Ulsterbus Tours for G8 work, then to Antrim, Armagh, Bangor, Coleraine, Larne and Newtownards from the following week. No 601, based at Antrim depot, is seen here in Belfast on 9 July 2013, covering for a Coleraine vehicle which had failed when on *Goldline* service 218.

At the end of 2014, the newest buses in the Ulsterbus fleet were 25 Optare Solo M925SRs delivered during October and allocated to Coleraine, Foyle (Derry~Londonderry), Larne, Lisburn and Newtownabbey. Like the Optare Versa V1170s delivered to Metro, these Solos came in a one-colour 'livery', an uninspired allover blue in this case. Here we see 1937, on the Foyle allocation, turning into Water Street en route to the city service stops on Foyle Street.

GOLDLINE

Translink doesn't always get it right – the 55-seat Rural buses featured elsewhere in the book, with their 3+2 seating, and regular misuse on urban and interurban services is a very good example – but sometimes it does. Look at what has happened on the *Goldline* network, introduced by Ted Hesketh back in 1990. The network of Ulsterbus *Express* services was enhanced then with higher specification vehicles branded as Ulsterbus *Goldliner*, the first coaches so liveried being 16 12m Leyland Tigers with Alexander 'TE' bodies. The success of the enhanced services was such that additional vehicles were required so passengers have since had the luxury of Volvo B10Ms with Plaxton Premiere and Excalibur coachwork, Volvo B10M/Van Hool articulated coaches, Irizar Intercentury-bodied Scania K94s, MAN/Ayats Bravo 1 double-deckers, Scania K320s with Irizar i4 coachwork and, most recently, Scania K400s with Irizar i6 63-seat bodywork. The number of journeys on most routes has been increased, there now being, for example, 12 peak hour departures from Larne between 06:15 and 09:00 each morning Monday to Friday and the *Maiden City Flyer* service between Belfast and Derry~Londonderry runs every fifteen minutes in the evening peak!

The last of the 16 Alexander 'TE'-bodied Leyland Tigers to remain in service was No 524, which was new at Magherafelt in May 1990 and spent almost its entire service there. Transferred on paper to the Driving School in late Summer 2007, it wasn't actually used there, but was returned to service at Ballymena. In this picture, dated 11 August 2007, No 524 was working from Cookstown on *Goldline* service 210 and is leaving the Europa Bus Centre on the 17:10 departure.

Top left: Volvo B10M/Plaxton Premiere 320 No 1603 was allocated to Belfast's Great Victoria Street depot in March 1996, primarily for use on services 200, 212 and 273. However, on this occasion in May 2005, it was performing a turn on service 300, which links Belfast and the International Airport at Aldergrove. It was photographed in Royal Avenue. When downgraded from *Goldline* duty, many of the vehicles in this batch were converted to 69-seat schoolbuses.

Top right: In May 1994, two Volvo B10MA/Van Hool 79-seat coaches, then numbered 3000/1, entered service with Citybus on the *CityExpress* service. They were later transferred to Ulsterbus, both ultimately ending up at Larne. No 3001, re-numbered 3111 to avoid a clash with Northern Ireland Railways' CAF diesel railcars was always thought the better of the pair having been at Larne longer. It was photographed on 21 May 2010 when operating the 15:00 Belfast (Europa Bus Centre) to Larne service 256. The destination is showing 'via Larne and Antrim Coast 252'; during the season, this departure operated as a connection for a Coleraine bus which left Larne for the Antrim Coast at 16:15. No 3111 is now in the fleet of Morton, Little London, Hampshire, has been re-registered H15 BUS and is painted in a very smart metallic green livery.

Left: No 3112, originally 3002, worked at Londonderry from new in May 1996 until withdrawal in June 2013. Along with sister 3113, new at Newry, but later transferred to Derry, the pair spent most of their time on service 212, the *Maiden City Flyer*, between Derry and Belfast. Forays elsewhere were rare, but on 22 May 2009, No 3112 put in an appearance on service 234 between Londonderry and the University of Ulster campus at Coleraine. (*John Durey*)

Right: With Belfast's Albert Memorial Clock in the background, completed in 1869 and standing at 113'0", Volvo B10M/Plaxton Excalibur No 1635, dating from September 1999, turns from High Street into Bridge Street as it departs the city for its home depot at Coleraine on 27 August 2011. The Farset river, from which Belfast derives its name, flows under High Street to reach the River Lagan. The clock tower was built on wooden piles and, as can be seen, has developed a list. In recent years the tower has been stabilised by substantial underpinning work.

Below: The next coaches for *Goldline*, in Autumn 2003, were 46 Scania K94s with Irizar Intercentury C53F coachwork. Ballymena-based No 1693 is seen climbing out of Belfast on the M2 motorway on the 14:50 departure from the Europa Bus Centre on 9 August 2007. On arrival at Ballymena, this duty then worked service 173 to Coleraine, returning to Belfast on *Goldline* 218 at 18:00 and back to Ballymena on a 219 at 19:50.

More of the Scania/Irizar combination arrived between September 2005 and January 2006. This is No 1732, passing The Nook, just at the entrance to the Giant's Causeway visitor centre. On this occasion, 25 May 2013, No 1732 wasn't engaged on *Goldline* work, but the more mundane local service 172 between Coleraine and Ballycastle via the scenic North Antrim coast.

The success of the *Goldline* operation, and the *Maiden City Flyer* between Londonderry and Belfast in particular, saw the introduction between June 2006 and January 2007 of 25 wheelchair accessible MAN ND363F/Ayats Bravo 1 double-deck coaches across the network. No 2006 was photographed on 3 March 2014 turning from Nelson Street, Belfast, onto Dunbar Link, near the end of its 75-mile journey on *Goldline* service 212 from Derry. Note the registration, AXI 296, transferred from a Leyland Leopard.

Left: The next order for single-deck coaches, in 2008, brought a new body supplier, Sunsundegui. Downpatrick depot received three of these Volvo B12Bs with Sunsundegui Sideral C53FL coachwork, featuring side-mounted wheelchair lifts, for service 215 to Belfast and service 240 to Newry/Dublin. No 1783 was photographed leaving the bus station at the seaside town of Newcastle on 9 March 2011 en route to Downpatrick.

Right: Seventeen months later and 14 of these Volvos, Nos 1772-4/6-86, could be found working in London on hire to Stagecoach UK Bus Events Limited in connection with the Olympic and Paralympic Games. Among that list was No 1780 from Derry. Note that all reference to Translink, Ulsterbus and *Goldline* has been covered over. *(Raymond Bell)*

For its 2012 *Goldline* coaches, Ulsterbus returned to the Scania/Irizar combination, this time on the K320 and with i4 C51FL coachwork. Like the Volvo/Sunsundegui combination, these feature a side-mounted lift for wheelchair access. The i4s are WiFi-fitted and the 51 seats are trimmed in E-leather. Ulsterbus contracted 90 vehicles to the London Organising Committee of the Olympic Games (LOCOG), including all 35 of the Scania K320/Irizar i4 coaches, Nos 1001-35. In fact, 34 of them, including No 1031 illustrated, were delivered direct from the coachbuilder to London where they were certified by staff from the Driver and Vehicle Agency Northern Ireland. In line with contract requirements, no branding was carried. It was a moment of great pride for Translink when 12 of the coaches were used to convey guests from Buckingham Palace to the opening ceremony at Olympic Park. *(Raymond Bell)*

While the first 35 i4 *Goldliners* were in London, Irizar in Spain was finishing another 13, which were delivered to Northern Ireland in time to take up duty from early September. Seen at the High Street/Bridge Street junction in Belfast within days of entering service is Larne depot's No 1046 on the 16:00 Belfast (Europa Bus Centre) to Larne service 256.

Below: The order for the Scania K320/Irizar i4 was extended again, with a further 30 vehicles delivered between December 2012 and March 2013. Coleraine depot's No 1063 was photographed on a delightful, Spring afternoon passing through the Co Antrim coastal village of Glenarm when working the morning southbound service on the seasonal *Antrim Coaster*, one of the UK's great bus rides. (*Noel O'Rawe*)

Left: The longest (rigid) vehicles used on the *Goldline* network are the nine tri-axle Scania K400/Irizar i6 C63FL coaches delivered between December 2012 and February 2013. Six, Nos 2051–6, are allocated to Great Victoria Street for the Dublin service (jointly operated with Bus Éireann, which normally uses VDL Synergy double-deckers), with three at Londonderry for services 212 (Belfast) and X4/274 (Dublin). No 2053 was photographed at the Europa Bus Centre on 15 February 2013, just a few days after entering service.

SCHOOLRUN, HIGH CAPACITY

A large part of Ulsterbus' work is the carriage of schoolchildren on contracts from schools and the Education and Library Boards. As a result, a fleet of high capacity buses has been built up, some new, some converted.

Thursday 18 April 2013 was a significant day in the history of Leyland bus operation in Northern Ireland when the fleet available for service reduced to just a single example. That bus was No 1489, allocated to Downpatrick, ostensibly for service 15a to Belfast via Annacloy and Kilmore where a weak bridge precludes the use of anything heavier. The penultimate Tiger in service was one of the 64-seat versions, No 1440, then based at Great Victoria Street, but which had been new at Coleraine in September 1992, spending several years working from the outstation at Kilrea. No 1440 is shown here leaving Crumlin on 18 April 2013 on the 15:35 service 106 to Belfast via Hannahstown and, ultimately, withdrawal.

Top left: If the *Goldline* service to Dublin and the Belfast International Airport service are ignored, most of the rest of the work at Ulsterbus' Great Victoria Street depot is schools rather than service, and across a wide area of Greater Belfast, too. Back on 15 April 2008, Volvo B10M/Alexander 'Q' No 1537 leaves to take up a journey from one of the many west Belfast schools.

Top right: No 1604 is a Volvo B10M with Plaxton Premiere 320 coachwork. Delivered new in January 1996 for the *Goldline* fleet, it was converted to a 69-seat bus for schools services in February 2007. It was unique amongst those so converted in being fitted with an LED destination display and flashing wig-wag lights, as the prototype for the Wright Eclipse SchoolRun-bodied Volvo B7Rs which were to follow. No 1604 was photographed leaving Belfast on 17 February 2011 on the 15:30 service 109 from the Europa Bus Centre to Antrim via Lisburn and Crumlin. In January 2013, No 1604 passed to the Londonderry and Lough Swilly Railway Company as its No 561 and was re-registered 96 DL 11328 (see page 17).

Left: Two hundred and twenty Volvo B7Rs with Wright bodies (Nos 180-359, 361-400) entered the Ulsterbus fleet between June 2007 and May 2010; No 360 was delivered to Citybus, albeit in Ulsterbus livery, to replace Leyland Tiger No 361. Photographed near Dromore (the Co Tyrone one) on 13 April 2011 when en route to Enniskillen, is Omagh depot's Volvo B7R/Wright Eclipse SchoolRun No 301. The seating capacity of the Wright Eclipse SchoolRun body varies between 62 and 66; the 66-seaters have four seats which can be removed for the carriage of a wheelchair, access being via a side-mounted lift. *(Paul Rafferty)*

Top left: Loughguile is in North Antrim and has a regular, if infrequent, service to Ballymoney provided by Ulsterbus (service 133), and, prior to 28 March 2015, more frequently by Logan, Dunloy. There are also school buses to Ballymena and Ballycastle. On 28 October 2011, No 384, technically a High Capacity model rather than a SchoolRun, has set down passengers at Loughguile chapel and is ready to depart for Cloughmills then Ballymena depot. Although the bus on this journey shows Corkey as the destination, the service runs to Loughguile, where it turns and heads back to Corkey, thence to Cloughmills via Ballyweaney and Ballyveeley Roads. *(Noel O'Rawe)*

Top right: Mercedes-Benz O405GN No 3103 was transferred to Derry on 27 January 2012 for use on schools services. Its seating capacity had been increased from 59 to 67 by replacing the dual-purpose seats previously fitted with bus seats removed from withdrawn Volvo B10Ls. It was withdrawn at the commencement of the 2013 school summer holidays.

Left: In early 2011, Scania K94/Irizar Intercentury No 1662 was deemed surplus to *Goldline* requirements and was selected to be the prototype for the next generation of conversions to high-capacity school buses. Using seats from withdrawn Volvo B10M/Plaxton Premiere No 1612, No 1662 was fitted out with 69 bus seats, in 3+2 configuration. It was also painted out of *Goldline* livery into the Ocean Blue and grey bus scheme. On a damp evening in October 2013, Larne depot's similarly treated No 1699 waits time in Belfast's High Street before taking up the 16:50 service 253 to Ballyclare. The destination 'Grammar School' indicates that it had worked into the city on a school run from Ballyclare.

RURAL BUSES

Ulsterbus had been used to its Leyland Leopards and Tigers, which seated either 49 or 53 passengers, making them suitable for either schools or service work. The substantially lower seating capacity of a low floor bus, and requirements to have children seated on schools journeys, led the company to develop a low floor, wheelchair accessible, rural bus, with 55 seats, some in 3+2 format. Forty-five of each of two types were ordered, the Volvo B7RLE with Alexander Dennis Enviro 300 body (Nos 501-45) and the Scania K230 with Wright Solar Rural body (Nos 401-45).

Funding for additional new buses in 2010 resulted in forty-eight more Scania K230s with Wright Solar Rural bodies joining the fleet, numbered 446-93. Seen at Attical, in the High Mournes, on 19 August 2014, is Newcastle-allocated No 464, displaying branding for the seasonal circular *Mourne Rambler* service, which links Newcastle with Tollymore Forest Park, Spelga Dam, the Silent Valley reservoir and various mountain paths. On Tuesdays to Fridays, the *Mourne Rambler* connects at Attical with the *Kilkeel Rambler* between that fishing port and the mountain hamlet (see also p70).

Early on the fine summer's morning of 28 June 2011, Omagh depot's No 560, from the third batch of Scania/Wright 'rural' buses, heads south towards Fivemiletown on service 85 to pick up its school run back to Omagh. Wheelchair access on all of the 'rural' buses is via a second door located behind the front axle. *(Paul Rafferty)*

Top left: Ballymena-based No 543 is an example of the 45 Volvo B7RLE/Alexander Dennis Enviro 300 Rural buses. On Saturday 31 August 2013, it was found at Ballymoney, at the head of a line of buses on demonstration specials for a Royal Black Institution parade.

Top right: A most unusual allocation to service 252 the *Antrim Coaster* on Saturday 21 July 2012 was Coleraine depot's Volvo B7RLE No 530, seen at Cushendun at 17:35 waiting the southbound bus and a change of driver. Normally the preserve of Scania K94/Irizar Intercentury *Goldliners*, this working was due to a wheelchair-bound passenger being carried earlier in the day. The Larne driver, who brought the bus north, would have been unfamiliar with the type as the 'Rural' allocation at that depot is the Scania/Wright version. *(Noel O'Rawe)*

FOYLESIDE SNOW

2010 saw Londonderry blanketed in snow in both January and December. In January, it was so cold that the River Foyle froze upstream of the Craigavon Bridge. However, the company and its staff attempted to keep services running for as long as possible as this selection of pictures shows.

A popular bus type with Derry drivers is the Wright Renown-bodied Volvo B10BLE, such as No 2842 seen here between the frost-laden trees on the Foyle Road on Saturday 9 January. No 2842 was new at Pennyburn garage, Derry in February 2000.

Left: In early December, the snow returned with a vengeance. During a snowstorm on 6 December Optare Solo No 1903, with Driver Michael McCusker at the wheel, struggles up Glendermott Road on city service FY3 to Kilfennan. It took Michael over an hour and a half to reach this spot on the inbound journey, a trip which would under normal conditions take twenty to twenty-five minutes. *(Stephen Baxter)*

Below: About the same time on the other side of the Foyle, Volvo B12B/ Sunsundegui Sideral No 1778 leaves the city's Foyle Street Bus Centre for Pennyburn garage. *(John Durey)*

Eleven days later and snow was again causing problems, with most services suspended. By 21:25, Driver Ken Simpson, driving Volvo B9TL/ Wright Eclipse Gemini No 2243, seen at Waterside railway station awaiting the arrival of a train from Belfast, was the only driver working in the Maiden City. *(Stephen Baxter)*

By 19 December the snow was still thick on the ground, but services were being maintained. Here we see Volvo B10BLE No 2838 on the slippy roads of Derry suburb Gobnascale. *(John Durey)*

ULSTERBUS TOURS

The Tours division is based at the Europa Bus Centre, Belfast, and operates a year-round programme of coach holidays throughout the British Isles and into Continental Europe. It also provides a day tours programme, excursions to various sporting events and coaches for high profile private hires. Consequently, the fleet normally receives three or four replacement coaches each year, with the older vehicles either being cascaded to local depots, or sold. It also has responsibility for the joint services with National Express and Scottish Citylink.

Top: Ulsterbus Tours' Stranraer depot provides coaches and drivers for the cross-channel express services from the ferry ports on Loch Ryan to Manchester/Birmingham/London and Glasgow/Edinburgh. At Stranraer Harbour on 27 May 2006, Volvo B10M/Plaxton Excalibur No 1659 has arrived with service 921 from Birmingham, where it left eight and a half hours previously. In late 2014, No 1659 could be found in Belfast, working for Belfast Bus Company.

Ten and a half months earlier, on 12 July 2005, Scania K114/Irizar Century No 109 waits at Stranraer Harbour for the Stena Line high speed service to arrive from Belfast. Departing at c19:45, the 920 service to London would call at towns and villages through Dumfries and Galloway, then Carlisle, Manchester and Birmingham, before reaching London around 06:00 the following morning, by then in the hands of a National Express driver, the Stranraer-based Ulsterbus man having come off at Birmingham. Repainted into fleet livery in 2007, No 109 was withdrawn in March 2010, with the arrival of Scania K360s Nos 130-2, and sold to Plaxton (dealer), Anston.

For the 2008 season, Ulsterbus Tours ordered four of these Sunsundegui Sideral-bodied coaches. They differed from the *Goldline* version, on the rear-engined Volvo B12B chassis, by being on the mid-engined Volvo B12M. For reasons which have never been made clear, though believed to have been problems with certification, they never entered service and were returned to Volvo, where they lay unsold for several years. After modifications were undertaken, they were sold to operators in Great Britain.

Below: In April 2009, Mercedes-Benz O814D/ Plaxton Cheetah Nos 3 and 4 were sold to Plaxton (dealer). This picture, taken at 14:55 on 8 April, shows No 3 in Belfast's Great Victoria Street en route to the ferry port for shipping to Great Britain.

Ayats Bravo No 2001 was delivered new to Citybus in December 1999 for use on its city tours programme. Just over three years later it transferred to Ulsterbus for use on the *Goldline* network. As the years went by, its use on express services reduced, it spending more time on schools duties at its home base, Derry. For the 2010 Summer season, it transferred back to Belfast to work a multi-lingual city tour programme, Translink City Sights, for Ulsterbus Tours, the English language commentary being prepared by driver Tom McWilliams. Withdrawn in 2013, it's now working for an operator in the Republic of Ireland.

The Tours fleet had changed from AEC Reliances to Leyland Leopards then Tigers, on to DAF MB230s then to Volvo B10Ms, with coachwork by Duple, Plaxton and Caetano. The 2002 seaswon saw another change, with the first deliveries of the Scania/Irizar combination. Four Scania K114EBs, with Spanish-built Irizar Century C49Ft coachwork, Nos 100-3, entered service in May, operating on the Company's continental tours. Two and a half years later, on 1 December 2004, No 100 is seen here at the Deutsches Eck, Koblenz, Germany, where the rivers Rhine and Moselle meet. No 100 was withdrawn in 2014 and sold to Scania (dealer).

For some years Volvo B10M-62/Caetano Enigma 696, which had been new in May 2001, had been second fiddle to Volvo B12B/Plaxton Panther No 114 for the tours operated from Londonderry under the Ulsterbus Tours Northwest banner. It was withdrawn for disposal in November 2014 and replaced with Volvo B12B/Plaxton Panther No 112, new in June 2005, transferred from Belfast.

As noted in the previous caption, for the 2005 season, the Tours fleet received four Volvo B12Bs with Plaxton Panther 49-seat coachwork. No 115 is seen here in Germany, at Cochem, by the Moselle, on 4 December 2005.

Top left: The next purchases, in 2006, were also of the Volvo/Plaxton combination, this time on the B12M. These four coaches, Nos 116-9, were longer than the previous B12Bs, but had only 48, leather-trimmed, seats, giving passengers more legroom, beneficial on long European tours. The photographer gets a cheery wave from the driver of No 116 as a tour leaves the Giant's Causeway on 17 September 2011.

The Stranraer-based cross-channel express services fleet received an upgrade in November 2006 with the delivery of four Volvo B12Bs, with Plaxton Panther 49-seat coachwork. All four, Nos 120–3, feature wheelchair lifts in the (wider) front entrance and were delivered in Eurolines livery for the Belfast to Birmingham (921) and London (920) services. These vehicles also worked a London (Victoria Coach Station)–Dover–London round trip during their layover in London. In late November 2011, No 120 (left) was painted in Scottish Citylink livery for operation on the joint service from Stranraer to Glasgow/Edinburgh, which calls at Stena Line's Loch Ryan Port, Cairnryan, to uplift passengers from Northern Ireland. It's seen here at Great Victoria Street depot fresh from Duncrue Street Works. No 122 (top right) is the only one of the four to receive the current National Express livery of white with grey stripes to the rear. It has worn this scheme since mid-2010.

The 2009 season touring coaches were to be the biggest ever purchased. Six tri-axle Scania K420EB/Irizar PBs, numbered 124-9, took up duty in May that year and were given three digit registrations removed from withdrawn Leyland Leopards. On 18 August 2009, No 129, then the charge of Driver Sammy Millar, was photographed in the Alps returning from a tour to the Italian Lakes. The coaches seat just 52 passengers in the 14.4m bodies. *(Trevor Dixon)*

Seen leaving Stranraer Harbour on the heavily delayed morning 923 service to Glasgow/Edinburgh on 19 November 2011, the penultimate day of shipping operations at the port, is anonymous No 123, the only indication of ownership by Ulsterbus being on the legal address.

In the late winter of 2009/10, three new Scania K360/Irizar Century coaches were delivered for National Express work from Stranraer depot. These were numbered 130-2 and the Irizar bodies featured a side-mounted wheelchair lift. No 130 is seen at the Europa Bus Centre on 25 February 2010, when presented for inspection by Ulsterbus Tours' management.

By the summer of 2014, Nos 130-2 were looking rather less tidy, all running in anonymous white, with just small Ulsterbus Express names appended. No 132, en route for Stranraer from Edinburgh, is seen leaving Stena Line's Loch Ryan Port on 9 July, having just set down its Belfast-bound passengers.

Top left: 2011's delivery of Tours coaches was again the tri-axle Scania/Irizar combination, this time the K400EB with Irizar's new i6 coachwork. August 2013 saw Belfast host the World Police and Fire Games, for which Ulsterbus Tours was an Official Excursions Partner and Official Coach Hire Partner. Scania K400EB/Irizar i6 No 134, which had previously carried a livery promoting Titanic Belfast visitor experience and the new visitor centre at the Giant's Causeway, in early July received vinyls promoting the Games, red/orange on the offside and two shades of green on the nearside.

Top right: For the 2014 season, four more Scania K360/Irizar i6 coaches were purchased for the Tours fleet. Numbered 139-42 (SFZ 9139-42), these were re-seated from C53Ft to C49Ft prior to entering service, though this change resulted in a rather untidy interior layout, with uneven spacing of seats. No 140 is seen departing Donegall Square West, Belfast, when engaged on private hire work.

Below: At the beginning of August 2013, the fleet of coaches based at Stranraer, for use on the cross-channel express services operated jointly with National Express and Scottish Citylink, was upgraded with the entry into service of three Scania K360s with Irizar i6 coachwork. The i6 body already featured in both the Tours and *Goldline* fleets, but on the three-axle version of the Scania K400. These three feature 49 seats, a toilet in the offside rear corner and a side-mounted wheelchair lift. No 136 (NFZ 9136), shown here outside the garage at Stranraer on 9 July 2014, had arrived on the overnight service from London (Victoria Coach Station).

FLEXIBUS

Flexibus Limited was formed in 1984 using the existing legal framework of Coastal Bus Services Limited, Portrush, which had been taken over by Ulsterbus Limited in 1974 and retained as a dormant subsidiary since, to develop a new market for small coach private hire, contract operations and new services where the use of a full size vehicle wouldn't be viable. By 2008, there was no need for such a 'low cost' unit, so the remaining operations of Flexibus Limited were transferred to Citybus (Metro) at Short Strand.

Many years after closure, Belfast City Council redeveloped the site of its gasworks on Cromac Street with new office and business units and an hotel. As this site is on the edge of the city centre, the Council provided a Monday to Friday shuttle service for staff and visitors. This was provided by Flexibus and by May 2007, Dennis Dart SLF/Wright Crusader No 641 had been given this livery as the dedicated bus.

No 917, a Mercedes-Benz 711D with Alexander 'AM' bodywork was one of a group of 30 new to Ulsterbus in 1996, taking fleet numbers 893-922. Initially used on *Busybus* town routes in Larne, No 917 moved to the Flexibus fleet in October 2005, staying until the run-down of that operation in 2008. It was sold to its present owner Henry (JMB Coaches), Cookstown, via Wilson's Auctions, Mallusk. It is shown in Donegall Place, Belfast, on 3 August 2007, when that thoroughfare was still two-way, still in *Busybus* livery.

Top left: A number of the Mercedes-Benz 711Ds transferred to the Flexibus operation received a new livery. One such was No 920, new in March 1996 and transferred from Ulsterbus in August 2005. In this August 2008 view, just a few weeks before the closure of the Flexibus operation, No 920, also in Donegall Place, is working a park and ride service.

Top right: The newest vehicles in the Flexibus fleet in the Summer of 2008 were nine Optare Solo M850s delivered between November 2002 and March 2003, an example being No 1834, which transferred to Citybus in September with the Flexibus operation.

Right: Dennis Dart SLF/Wright Crusader No 642 was delivered new to Citybus in February 1997 for use on the *Easibus* network of accessible services. Taken out of service in February 2006, it was held in reserve until painted blue and transferred to Flexibus in April 2008. In July of that year it was on the move again, this time to Ulsterbus Dungannon where it would remain until withdrawn the following year. It's seen here in Belfast's Royal Avenue in use on the Northside Park and Ride contract, just three months before the closure of the Flexibus operation at the end of August 2008.

SPECIAL SERVICES

In this section we look at buses which have had branding applied for specific services. However, as will become obvious, Translink companies are not good at ensuring those buses actually work where they're supposed to.

Above: In September/October 2005, Great Victoria Street depot received ten Alexander ALX400-bodied Volvo B7TLs. Nos 2994 and 2995 were allocated to service 300 between Belfast city centre and Belfast International Airport and received minimal branding on fleet livery. No 2994 is seen here passing the entrance to the Castle Upton estate, at Templepatrick, in June 2006.

Left: Also at Templepatrick in June 2006, and with similar branding applied, is Scania L94/Wright Solar No 823. Nos 819-24 were allocated to Great Victoria Street for the International Airport route and so were fitted with luggage racks and, later, automated, multi-lingual, next stop announcements.

Top left: Similar, though subtly different, branding was applied to several Scania L94s delivered to Antrim depot in August 2006. Intended for service 109a, linking Antrim with Lisburn via Belfast International Airport, when photographed on 19 May 2012 No 836 was in use from Crumlin depot on Citystopper 523 between Belfast and Lisburn city centres.

Top right: The airport services branding was later applied to the Citybus Optare Solo M850s used on the Belfast city centre to George Best Belfast City Airport service, though when photographed on 15 September 2010, No 1835 was actually in use on service 95 to the Royal Hospitals.

Left: In September 2009, the Optare Solos allocated to the George Best Belfast City Airport route, Nos 1835-7, were replaced with newer, longer, M920 examples, Nos 1881/97/8, transferred in from Ulsterbus. Wearing its new coat of magenta, Citybus No 1897 heads for the airport on 15 September.

Optare Solo M920SLs Nos 1913-5 were transferred to Citybus in May 2006 for use on the Black's Road Park and Ride service, though weren't repainted and had minimal branding applied to the Ulsterbus livery, so minimal that No 1914, photographed at the Durham Street/Glengall Street junction on 15 April 2008, still claims to be an Ulsterbus!

Of the ten Volvo B7TLs allocated to Great Victoria Street, Nos 2990-3 were for the Park and Ride service along the M1 motorway to Sprucefield, though, when photographed in Great Victoria Street on 5 July 2011, No 2992 was in use on the 15:00 Belfast city centre to Lisburn Citystopper service 530. It would, at least, pass close to the Park and Ride site at Black's Road, though not stop.

In November 2010, to coincide with the opening of a new Park and Ride site at Cairnshill on the southern approach to Belfast, from the Downpatrick/Newcastle direction, a smart, green livery began to be applied to 'dedicated' park and ride buses, though it didn't take long for them to start to wander.

Above: Although smartly branded for the 650 service to the Park and Ride site at Black's Road, when photographed on 6 June 2011, No 1915 was actually in use on service 600 to George Best Belfast City Airport. What sort of impression do visitors get when arriving at the airport to be met by a bus in the wrong colour and advertising the wrong destination?

Right: Scania L94/Wright Solar No 2415 was transferred from Newcastle to Great Victoria Street and smartly repainted in the green livery for the introduction of the Cairnshill Park and Ride service. However, it could just as often be found working elsewhere, such as on 28 June 2011 when it was in use on the 15:30 service 300 to Belfast International Airport when photographed turning from High Street into Bridge Street, Belfast. Similar buses Nos 2412-4, allocated to Ballynahinch, also received the green livery.

Left: Four of the 2007 Volvo B9TL/Wright Eclipse Geminis, Nos 2227-30, also wear the green scheme for the Cairnshill Park and Ride route. Nos 2227/8/30 were allocated to Ballynahinch, while No 2229, seen passing through Donegall Square North in front of Belfast City Hall on 26 July 2011, was then working from Great Victoria Street, though since transferred to join its sisters at Ballynahinch. In an all too common occurrence, it wasn't on the Cairnshill route, but that to Belfast International Airport!

Below: Two of the double-deckers on the Sprucefield route were replaced with Scania K230/Wright Solar Rural Nos 571/2. Obviously no-one in Translink's senior management team or Marketing Department has ever travelled on one of these vehicles, with their cramped 3+2 seating, else they would never have been allocated to this prime route. Such unsuitable vehicles will never tempt BMW drivers out of their luxury cars! When photographed on 4 May 2011, No 572 was heading in the opposite direction to Sprucefield, to Belfast International Airport, in fact.

Top left: Two of the four Volvo B7TL/ Alexander ALX400s allocated to the Sprucefield Park and Ride service, Nos 2990/2, were given the green scheme. Seen in Donegall Square North on 9 January 2012, No 2990 is working the same journey to Lisburn as No 2992 illustrated earlier.

Top right: Having been operated by Volvo B10BLE/Wright Renowns Nos 2774-6 for most of September 2014, on Monday 6 October the three Optare Versa V1170 43-seaters delivered in the green scheme took over on the Black's Road route. No 1810 looks very smart as it lays over at Great Victoria Street depot between runs.

Right: 1 December 2014 saw the opening of a new park-and-ride site at Dunlady Road, Dundonald, which was served at peak hours by a new, limited stop, Metro service numbered 4x. As noted in the Metro section, Volvo B5TL No 2196, at least, had received a coat of the usual park-and-ride green, but by the time it was delivered it was in magenta. Similar No 2198, like No 2196, entered service on Monday 1 December, in standard fleet magenta. However, by the following Saturday it had gained this magenta-based allover scheme for the new Park and Ride site. It does seem odd that, in times of financial constraint, a bus can be painted, full vinyls and advertising applied, be repainted before it enters service then, within days, another bus, which entered service on the same day, can have a different allover advert, with the same message, applied.

A new livery for the Belfast airports services was developed in 2011.

Top left: The Scania L94s on the Belfast International Airport route had accumulated high mileages and in April 2011 were replaced with eight Scania K230/Wright Solar Rurals, numbered 551-5, in a dark blue livery. These differ internally from the rest of the Solar Rural fleet as they have luggage racks, fewer seats and more legroom, but for reasons known only to those who specified them still have two rows of 3+2 schoolbus-type seating to the rear of the saloon. No 555 is shown at Nelson Street, Belfast, on 3 March 2014 on a journey from the airport.

Top right: The pair of Volvo B7TLs on airport duty, Nos 2994/5, also received the dark blue livery. A downside for the use of these vehicles on the motorway route is that they are restricted to 50 mph because of the tyres fitted.

Left: While I have seen Metro's airport-liveried Optare Solos operate on Park and Ride duties and the Royal Hospitals service, only once have I seen one on 'normal' service, that being on 10 August 2011 when No 1881 put in a peak-hour appearance on long route 64a to Fairview Road, Carnmoney. Either a Volvo B10BLE or a Scania L94 would have been the normal fayre for this journey.

The Eastside and Northside Park and Ride services in Belfast city centre are operated on behalf of the Department for Regional Development, and differ from those mentioned previously in that users pay for parking then get a free bus trip.

Left: The Dennis Darts which had operated on the Eastside and Northside Park and Ride services, Nos 645/7 (see Buses in Ulster Vol 6 *The Hesketh Years 1988-2003*, p86), were ultimately replaced by a pair of 2003 Optare Solo M850, Nos 1848/9, transferred from Ulsterbus in November 2009 and given the livery for the vehicles dedicated to these routes, 1848 becoming the Northside bus and 1849 the Eastside.

Right: The Summer of 2014 saw Optare Solos Nos 1848/9 replaced on the Eastside and Northside Park and Ride services by newer M920SL models Nos 1914/5. This second picture of No 1915 (see p102) shows it exiting Donegall Place on what is thought to be its first day in service in its new livery, Monday 11 August 2014.

The network of *Easibus* accessible services based on Connswater and Abbeycentre shopping centres has received new Optare Solos twice in the period reviewed.

Left: August 2005 saw the delivery to Metro of a quartet of Solo M920 models, Nos 1920-3, which received registration numbers from soon-to-be withdrawn Leyland Leopards. No 1923 was allocated to the Royal Hospitals service, while the others worked on *Easibus* and schools. In 2014, despite having been tested each year for nine years, it was discovered that Nos 1920/2 were carrying the wrong registration numbers, which were duly swapped. No 1920, by then re-registered VOI 205, ex-VOI 200, was photographed on 13 August arriving at Abbeycentre.

Below: November 2014 and a pair of Optare Solo M925SR models, Nos 1959/60, part of a Translink order for 27 such buses, arrived at Short Strand depot. Caught in the day's last rays of sunshine, No 1960 departs Connswater shopping centre for the Sydenham, Knocknagoney and Abbey Ring areas on 26 November 2014.

UP AT THE CAUSEWAY

One of the biggest attractions for visitors to Northern Ireland is the Giant's Causeway, on the north coast of Co Antrim, near Bushmills, famous in its own right for its distillery which has been producing whiskey since 1608.

For some years, the seasonal open-top service between Coleraine and the Giant's Causeway via the coastal route was maintained with elderly Leyland Atlantean/Eastern Coachworks No 4901, new to Yorkshire Woollen District in November 1979 and acquired by Ulsterbus, for schools work, in November 1989. In 1994, it was converted to a glass-topped observation coach for Citybus' Belfast city tours, but had several windows broken by stone-throwing idiots. It was then converted to part open-top and later transferred to Coleraine. This picture was taken at The Nook, by the entrance to the Causeway site, on 7 August 2010. No 4901, the last of a long line of Leyland double-deckers in the fleets of the state-owned transport operators in Northern Ireland, was sold for scrap in January 2014.

Left: The Giant's Causeway itself is some distance away from the visitor facilities and car parks, down a steep road. Ulsterbus provides a frequent service, the *Causeway Coaster*, along this road all year round. The turning area at the Causeway was particularly tight, precluding the use of Optare Solos, which is why Mercedes-Benz No 1814 (seen below) was retained as spare. To upgrade the service, and provide low floor, wheelchair accessibility, in May/June 2008, two Enterprise Plasma/Plaxton Primos were leased and numbered 001/2. Both were given a smart livery featuring a representation of the Causeway stones. No 001 is seen at the famous attraction on 13 July 2008.

Below: On 5 June 2010, one of the vehicles in use was Mercedes-Benz O814D/Wright Nimbus No 1814, then the spare vehicle. When new in June 1995, No 1814 was registered HAZ 5814, being re-registered AXI 314 in February 2006, before reverting to its original number in September 2006. It was sold in December 2012 to McLaughlin, Convoy, Co Donegal.

In November 2009, the pair of leased 2008 'Primos' was returned and two older, 2007, models were purchased and numbered 3 and 4. Both were re-registered in late Summer 2010 with numbers transferred from soon-to-be-withdrawn Leyland Tigers, No 3, seen below on 31 August 2010, becoming RXI 3333 and No 4 WXI 1400. They also received a new livery, to promote the National Trust's fundraising campaign, 'A Giant Cause'.

Right: For the 2013 season, Nos 3 and 4 were treated to a repaint in green. No 4 is seen here on the single track road between the visitors centre and the Causeway on 16 March 2013.

Left: The Giant's Causeway site is linked with other North Coast tourist sites by seasonal service 402, the *Causeway Rambler*, connecting Coleraine, Portrush, Dunluce Castle, Bushmills Distillery, the Giant's Causeway site and the rope bridge at Carrick-a-Rede, and regular local service 172 between Coleraine and Ballycastle. On 20 July 2013, one of the two buses on service 402 was Optare Solo No 1854, seen arriving at The Nook, to pick up visitors from the Causeway.

Below: It only took Ulsterbus until 2011 to acquire its first (and so far only) Olympian, when it purchased from Dublin Bus that company's Volvo Olympian/Alexander 'RH' No RV508 (99 D 508). Converted to part open-top layout, and fitted with a wheelchair ramp in the space where the exit door used to be, the Olympian, now numbered 2000 and registered CXI 6200, that number being transferred from the Ford recovery crane at Coleraine depot, took up its duties on the seasonal service 177 between Coleraine and the Giant's Causeway at the end of June that year. It's seen here at the Causeway stop on 23 July.

HERITAGE FLEET

With the foresight of some of the senior management team, three historic vehicles have been retained for a 'heritage fleet' and are available for private hire.

The oldest of the heritage trio is Bedford OWB No V957, new in 1942 and restored in Northern Ireland Road Transport Board livery. Built to wartime austerity specification, complete with wooden slatted seats, it ran until 1948 and was then sold to dealer SMT Sales & Service. It was rebodied by SMT with coachwork similar in appearance to Duple's Vista body (built under licence) and ran with a number of Scottish operators before ending its days as staff transport for a fruit farmer. Acquired by a Northern Ireland-based enthusiast in the mid 1970s for preservation, it was later purchased by Ulsterbus, which built a replica body to the original Scottish Motor Traction wartime utility specification.

One of a batch of 40 with bodies built at the Ulster Transport Authority's Duncrue Street Workshops in 1963, AEC Reliance No S234 went new on 9 April 1963 to Belfast's Smithfield Depot, although was often out-stationed at Whitehead. Its last three years of service with Ulsterbus were at Ballymena from where it was withdrawn and placed in Reserve on 1 September 1980. After several years in store it was taken into Duncrue Street Workshops, overhauled and restored to original UTA two-tone blue livery. It was then reinstated for special duties at Glengall Street, Belfast, on 1 July 1985. Further more recent attention given at Duncrue Street has included a full interior retrim and external repaint.

New to the Northern Ireland Road Transport Board on 31 May 1947, Leyland PS1 No A515 spent most of its life, the greater part of which was with the Ulster Transport Authority, allocated in the Lurgan/Portadown area. The final two and a half months of its service life was with Ulsterbus and on withdrawal on 30 June 1967 it became a tow-car for several years before passing into private preservation. In 1997 it was re-acquired by Ulsterbus for promotional work and continued preservation. In recognition of its unique heritage in being the only bus still in existence to have been used in passenger service with all three state-owned bus companies – NIRTB, UTA and Ulsterbus – a very thorough restoration was completed during 2007/8 at Duncrue Street Workshops to its 1950s UTA condition. It is seen here in Groomsport on 27 April 2013.

DESTRUCTION

It's sad that this section can be included in this volume as we'd all hoped the troubled days of Northern Ireland's past had gone. However, over the last decade, there have been several incidents of the hijacking and malicious destruction of vehicles. While we're looking at the vehicles here, we shouldn't forget the distress caused to the drivers who've been the victims of this foolishness.

Around tea-time on 4 August 2005, Citybus (Metro) Volvo B7TL/ Alexander ALX400 No 2927, new in April 2001, was hijacked at Woodvale Park, in the north of Belfast, and driven the short distance to Enfield Street, where it was set on fire. It was photographed early the following morning when there wasn't much left to recover. The plume of white smoke is coming from the diesel tank.

Just less than six weeks later, on 13 September, and just around the corner from where No 2927 was fired, Citybus (Metro) Scania L94/Wright Solar No 803 lies destroyed on Cambrai Street. It had been hijacked the previous night when returning to depot from Carr's Glen terminus.

The destruction of two Volvo B7TLs, Nos 2324 and 2998, at the Co Down village of Ballygowan overnight on 9/10 March 2007 appears to have been an act of wanton vandalism rather than anything to do with Northern Ireland's political situation. Both vehicles were relatively new, 2324 entering service in September 2006 and 2998 in September 2005.

Top left: On the evening of 25 October 2010, Citybus (Metro) Volvo B7TL/Alexander ALX400 No 2903 was hijacked at Rathcoole, Newtownabbey, to the north of Belfast, and driven across a grassy area onto O'Neill Road, almost onto the forecourt of a Texaco petrol station. The burned remains were recovered the following morning by local contractor Agnew using its specialised low-loader and crane. The next day, 27 October, Agnew's were back to the area to recover eight-week old Scania K230/Wright Solar Rural No 485, which had been hijacked and burned nearby at Cloughfern Corner.

Top right: In Derry, on 16 May 2011, to protest Her Majesty's Queen Elizabeth II's historic visit to the Republic of Ireland (which was happening almost 150 miles away!), Scania L94/ Wright Solar No 2405 was burned at Glengalliagh Road. It was recovered to Pennyburn garage by Agnew's and scrapped on site. (*Stephen Baxter*)

Right: The evening of Friday 11 January 2013, saw Citybus (Metro)/Volvo B7TL/Alexander ALX400 No 2918 became the third vehicle mentioned here to be destroyed in the Rathcoole/ O'Neill Road/Cloughfern area when it was taken and burned at Rathfern when being returned to Newtownabbey depot nearby. The location for this picture is just a few hundred yards from that of No 2903.

ENGINEERING SUPPORT

Over the years, Citybus and Ulsterbus have used a varied selection of converted buses for engineering support and attendance at breakdowns and accidents. Changes in legislation have seen the use of such vehicles diminish in recent years, with recovery work being contracted out to specialist providers, though several depots still retain a bus for yard shunting, while the engineers have a van for 'first response' attendance at roadside breakdowns. At the time of writing (mid-December 2014) just five buses – Leyland-engined Tigers 1238/60/70/92 and similar, but Volvo-engined, 1304 – remained tested.

An unusual recipient of Metro magenta and grey livery was Citybus (Metro) Leyland Leopard/Alexander towing vehicle No 1981. Based at Falls Park depot, No 1981 is seen here on 16 September 2009 entering Donegall Square North, Belfast, towing Volvo B10L/Alexander Ultra No 2714, which appears to have suffered a problem with its rear suspension.

On 12 July 2011, when the traditional Orange Order demonstration was being held that year at Holywood, Bangor-based Leyland Tiger No 1285 is seen parked in the car park at the railway station, as standby in case any of the demonstration specials required assistance.

The only Leyland Tiger/Alexander 'Q' type shortened and fitted out for engineering use is No 2640, seen here in Belfast on 13 April 2011 when its crew was en route to a failed Metro Volvo B10L/Alexander Ultra.

Coleraine depot engineers had the use of a Ford Cargo fitted with a Holmes crane. When seen on 25 June 2011, it had been given a coat of the latest Ocean Blue livery. It was still carrying registration CXI 6200, but, just a few days later, Volvo Olympian open-topper No 2000 took up duties carrying that number, the Ford becoming GFZ 7295. It has since been sold to an owner in Dundrum, Co Down.

Top: As mentioned in the introduction to this section, recovery work is now contracted out to specialist providers. Here, on 17 June 2010 on Belfast's College Avenue, we see Marsden's, Belfast, Volvo 520 recovery truck L777 MRS lifting Citybus (Metro) Volvo B10L/Alexander Ultra No 2729 in preparation for a tow home. *(Will Hughes)*

Left: This Mercedes 208CDi is typical of the vans used by depot engineers, though not all have received fleet colours.